The Food of Australia
Published by
Periplus Editions (HK) Ltd.
with editorial offices at
153 Milk Street
Boston, MA 02109
and
5 Little Road #08–01
Singapore 536983

ISBN: 962-593-393-X

Library of Congress Catalog
Card Number: 98–83180

Credits:
Food photographs by **Ashley Mackevicius**. All other
photography by **John Hay**, except pages 12, 15 & 24,
by **Esther Beaton**, Terra Australis Photo Agency, and
pages 13, 28 & 30 by **Glenn Gibson**, Blitz Pictures.

Acknowledgments
The publisher gratefully acknowledges the enthusiastic
support of Igal Bigos, Area Director, Food and Bever-
age Operations, of Hilton International Australia; his
assistant, Jacqui Fink, and Rod Ritchie of Rainforest
Publishing, who helped co-ordinate the project. The
publisher also wishes to thank all those who lent props
for photography, the contributing authors and, above
all, the enthusiastic and talented chefs who so gener-
ously shared their culinary secrets.

Distributed by

USA
Tuttle Publishing
Distribution Center
Airport Industrial Park
364 Innovation Drive
North Clarendon, VT 05759-9436
Tel: (802) 773-8930
Tel: (800) 526-2778

Japan
Tuttle Shokai Ltd.
1-21-13, Seki
Tama-ku, Kawasaki-shi
Kanagawa-ken 214-0022, Japan
Tel: (044) 833-0225
Fax: (044) 822-0413

Canada
Raincoast Books
8680 Cambie Street
Vancouver, British Columbia
V6P 6M9
Tel: (604) 323-7100
Fax: (604) 323-2600

Asia-Pacific
Berkeley Books Pte. Ltd.
5 Little Road #08-01
Singapore 536983
Tel: (65) 280-1330
Fax: (65) 280-6290

First Edition
1 3 5 7 9 10 8 6 4 2
06 05 04 03 02 01 00 99
PRINTED IN SINGAPORE

THE FOOD OF
AUSTRALIA

Contemporary Recipes from Australia's Leading Chefs

Stephanie Alexander	Guido van Baelen
Maggie Beer	Beh Kim Un
Andrew Blake	Marieke Brugman
Cheong Liew	Gerda Eilts
Andrew Fielke	Bethany Finn
Herbert Franceschini	Paul Hoeps
Werner Kimmeringer	Alan Koh
Kurt Looser	Christine Manfield
Bill Marchetti	Paul Merrony
Damien Pignolet	Dietmar Sawyer
Alla Wolf-Tasker	Tetsuya Wakuda

Produced in association with Hilton International Australia
Food photography by Ashley Mackevicius
Styling by Wendy Berecry & props by Christina Ong
Edited by Wendy Hutton

PERIPLUS

W

Contents

Part One: Food in Australia

The new "cuisine of the southern sun"

by Tony Baker

Australia's contemporary cuisine has, over the past fifteen years or so, joined the ranks of the world's best, thanks to the dazzling range of local ingredients, a truly multicultural society and a new generation of boldly creative chefs. It is a perfect drawing together of flavors and styles: of French traditional and *nouvelle cuisine*, regional Italian and pan-Asian styles laced with cool Californian chic.

The evolution of the new cuisine seems to have taken place with startling swiftness. To write about Australian food a couple of decades ago would have been to invite disbelief, if not downright laughter, together with derisive remarks about kangaroo and emu steaks. While it is true that within a month of Captain Cook sighting his first kangaroo in 1770, a member of his party had eaten one, for most of the next two centuries, Australians aped the cooking styles of England, a country many still thought of as home, and one not particularly renowned for fine cuisine. It is also true that until the past decade, the wild fruits, vegetables, nuts and seeds used for some 40,000 years by the Aborigines were totally ignored by the more recent Australian arrivals.

With the huge influx of immigrants in the years following World War II, a largely Anglo-Celtic society was enriched, first by Europeans, then by Asians, as well as immigrants from countries as diverse as Chile and Iran. Today, Australian tastes are as cosmopolitan and multicultural as its population.

Australians, perhaps the best-traveled nation in the world, have experienced firsthand the cuisines of Europe, Asia and America. So, too, have Australian chefs who, inspired by their experiences, have created a cuisine that benefits from the superb produce of this continental country, which produces everything from tropical fruits and herbs to cheese, wines and stunning seafood from the far south.

Australian cuisine emphasizes freshness and shows great creativity in successfully blending cuisines from as far apart as Paris and Tokyo. This new "cuisine of the southern sun" complements the relaxed friendliness of modern Australia, and is as likely to be enjoyed on a verandah or in a courtyard as in a formal dining room.

Wine is integral to Australian dining, since this happiest of revolutions has gone hand in hand with the discovery, both at home and abroad, that the fresh, clean, flavor-packed wines of Australia are comparable with—if not better than—those of the old wine world.

As if all this were not enough, by the standards of other gourmet cuisines Australian food is remarkably cheap, as increasing numbers of tourists are discovering to their delight.

Page 2.
From the Indian Ocean on the west to the Pacific Ocean on the east, the Australian continent is a land of contrasts.
Opposite:
All the elements for a fine picnic on the beach: seafood, cheese, salad and wine.

An Endless Feast

A continent full of superb fresh produce

by Tony Baker

From diamonds and gold to oil, Australia is exceptionally well endowed with natural resources. But for food lovers the greatest blessing is a range of climates, ranging from alpine to tropical. Add rich, ancient soils, some of the purest waters on the planet and guaranteed sunshine and the result is an endless feast of produce.

Visit any big city market and this national feast will be temptingly arrayed before you. Visit the various states and territories and you will be offered particularly local ways of preparing the regional specialities, from the mangoes and mud crabs of Queensland to the apples and farmed salmon of Tasmania.

Nowhere is this abundance more apparent than with Australian seafood, thanks to seas varying from warm to challengingly bracing, while the inland waterways contribute some unique crustaceans. To visit Queensland without tasting mud crabs and Moreton Bay bugs (similar to slipper or flathead lobsters) is to deprive yourself of two of life's intense pleasures. While you're there, you must also try

The cold waters of Tasmania, the island-state off the south of the Australian continent, are renowned for magnificent seafood, including succulent oysters.

such reef fish as red emperor, coral trout and pearl perch. In the Northern Territory as well as Queensland, barramundi fish, either large or small, is a must. Mention the Territory and you are reminded that Australian gourmets are increasingly partial to kangaroo, crocodile and buffalo. Traditional Territorians tuck into steaks that would embarrass folks in Argentina by their size. A popular local T-shirt has emblazoned on it the slogan "Eat beef, you bastards," a typically Australian approach to export promotion.

No visit to Sydney is complete without oysters and what Australians call "a feed of fish," such as John Dory or yellowfin tuna. Tasmania has a better than fair claim to being the seafood capital. The cool seas around this island state have long been prized for tasty deep-water fish, such as trevally and blue grenadier, not to mention rock lobster, giant deep-sea crabs and scallops. Without doubt, though, Tasmania's gift to the world's gourmets has been the salmon produced in recent years from its fish farms, avidly sought whether fresh, smoked or sugar-cured. Move around Australia pausing only for plates of fish such as snapper and the King George whiting (a South Australian delicacy, entirely unlike the northern hemisphere whiting), or the magnificent abalone, yabbies (freshwater crayfish) and a cascade of shrimp and you see why *sushi* bars have become so popular.

The same is true of fruit and nuts, as well as obvious joys such as mangoes, pineapples, pears and apples. The whole range of citrus—limes and mandarins and countless acres of oranges—are arrayed across the southeast Australian heartland. Berry fruits, grapes eaten fresh or dried into raisins and sultanas, apricots and peaches likewise fresh or dried, giant watermelons and nuts such as Australia's own buttery, crunchy macadamias abound. Think of a fruit and you can be sure that if it does not already exist in commercial quantities, an enthusiast is pioneering its production somewhere between the Indian and Pacific oceans.

In southern Australia, olive groves and the pressings from wild olives now yield oils as distinctive as those of Italy and Spain. Mention of those two countries is an instant reminder that the contribution of immigrants, mainly European and Asian, to the national feast has not been confined to restaurants and market gardens. Australian

Nuts range from walnuts grown on farms like this one in Milawa, northern Victoria, to macadamias, originally known as Queensland bush nuts and indigenous to Australia.

salamis and other processed meats are of exceptional quality because the meat is good and because Italian, German, Polish and other producers brought ancient skills to their new homes. Italian pasta makers showed the way. Today's pasta makers are likely to be fifth generation Australians, and one must not forget the first generation Chinese noodle makers.

When it comes to meat, Australians take quality and quantity for granted. The Sunday roast leg of lamb would be an Australian food cliché were it not so gorgeously juicy and intensely flavored, thanks to the lush well-watered pastures of southeast and southwestern Australia. Kangaroo meat has rapidly moved from pet food to an exotic delicacy to almost a staple. Close to a slightly gamey beef in taste, nutritionists like it for its low fat content. Emu meat

seems to be catching on the way kangaroo did; farmed venison is frequently found on menus and camel steaks have begun to make an appearance.

President Charles de Gaulle once said of his people: "The French will only be united under the threat of danger. Nobody can simply bring together a country that has 365 kinds of cheese." It won't be long before an Australian Prime Minister can make a similar remark.

Thanks to its sunshine and rainfall, Australia is perfect for dairying. Since the 1970s, when the missing element—the input of dedicated expert cheesemakers—was applied, the country began producing cheeses of international quality. Today, Australian gourmets avidly seek out the local products and cheese's share of the annual 500,000 tons of dairy exports is worth $1 billion in Australian currency.

Southern Australia has led the charge in producing superb cheese, particularly the offshore islands of Tasmania, King Island in Bass Strait and Kangaroo Island off South Australia. On the mainland, the main cheese states are New South Wales, Victoria, South Australia and Western Australia. Although generic names such as cheddar, brie and camembert are rife, there is an increasing trend to coin names which reflect their origin, like the splendidly Australian True Blue, or embrace the place of origin, such as Mersey Valley and Milawa Blue.

Whatever your cheese preference, it is made in Australia. And yes, there is at least one cheese flavored with gum leaves. Nor are Australia's cheeses confined to those from cow's and sheep's milk; there is a thriving goat's cheese industry making a range of products, including those hand-crafted

Opposite:
South Australia's Barossa Valley, settled initially by Germans, produces more than half of Australia's wine.
Left:
The lush pastures of southern Australia produce an excellent array of cheese.

by Kervella in Western Australia.

From sugar to salt, if it crosses the taste buds, it will be made in Australia. I have spent some time trying to think of something essential to a first-class chef's output that Australia does not produce. The only product which came to mind is the truffle and, as you read this, some earnest prospector is doubtless hunting through loamy Australian undergrowth in the hope of striking it fungus rich.

A History of Australian Cuisine

From food gathering to an appreciation of fine food

by Michael Symons

"Is this all men can do with a new country? Look at those tin cans!" In his documentary novel, *Kangaroo*, D.H. Lawrence repeatedly describes Australia as rusty tin cans scattered over bare ground. In 1923, he found "towns—and corrugated iron—and millions of little fences—and empty tins."

When Europeans invaded the continent just over two centuries ago, Australia went from the highly integrated food gathering practiced by the Aborigines to settled agriculture and grazing. This led to the sale of food in sacks and barrels, then bottles and cans, and finally to frozen and takeaway packs. Until recently, Australian food was the rapidly evolving cuisine of agribusiness, not a cuisine built on the love of fine food.

With the emergence of the grazing industry in the 19th century, bush workers were paid in rations called "Ten, Ten, Two & A Quarter" after the typical weekly issue of 10 pounds meat, 10 pounds flour, 2 pounds sugar and ¼ pound tea. In addition, the rations included salt and liquor. The meat, which had been salted pork or beef, became mutton slaughtered on the sheep station. Together, the rations provided a minimal diet which typically consisted of slabs of meat grilled on an open fire, heavy bread or "damper" baked in the ashes, overly sweetened tea boiled in a tin pot called a "billy," and drinks that were guzzled not for taste but for intoxication.

The reformer Caroline Chisholm tried to civilize the place by conducting a public campaign to attract married couples and, especially, single women as immigrants. She distributed a booklet in London in 1847 entitled *Comfort for the Poor! Meat Three Times a Day!!* Promising meat at every meal was a compelling advertising slogan.

Remarking on the central culinary paradox of the country, a young French journalist, Edmond Marin La Meslée, wrote in 1883: "No other country on earth offers more of everything needed to make a good meal, or offers it more cheaply, than Australia: but there is no other country either where the cuisine is more elementary, not to say abominable."

Rough bush eating habits were civilized through improvements in the food industry. Prior to that, investments had been largely directed at primary production, and this generally meant wool. This made Australia little more than a basic "garden," and entrepreneurs had to turn their hands to the next step in the production chain-food processing and preparation. In the second half of the 19th century, the excitement shifted to food preservation and distribution. An Australian, James Harrison, has been credited with inventing mechanical refrigeration in 1851, and its first use was in long-distance shipping. Massive investment in railways opened up the hinterland to the growing of wheat, milk, sugar, fruit and vegetables.

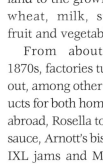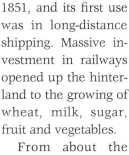

Schoolboys eating a typical lunch: a homemade Vegemite sandwich, a factory-made meat pie and a Chiko roll, a peculiarly local interpretation of the Chinese spring roll. Vegemite, a pungent spread made from yeast extract, is virtually an Australian icon.

From about the 1870s, factories turned out, among other products for both home and abroad, Rosella tomato sauce, Arnott's biscuits, IXL jams and MacRobertson's chocolates. Roller-mills produced the white flour that became so symbolic of mass-produced food. While much of the country had been too hot for traditional brewing, in 1888 the Fosters brothers brought from the United States the technology for bottled lager beer, which relied on refrigeration, pasteurization, bottom fermentation and bottling.

With this second great revolution (the industri-alization of food storage and distribution), Australian cooks advanced beyond the carcasses of meat, sacks of flour and chests of tea. They were encouraged to purchase packaged foods. In short, Australian households relied on those tin cans that caught the eye of D.H. Lawrence.

But from the 1890s, suburban housewives purchased local recipe books, even if they remained essentially rearrangements of Eliza Acton's *Modern Cookery for Private Families of England*, written a half-century earlier. Each city adopted its culinary "bible," produced by the local gas company or a fund-raising group.

Australian women excelled at plain and decent cookery, such as baked or roasted meats and vegetables. They also prided themselves on their puddings and cakes, relying on the iron kitchen range and the store cupboard's flour, sugar, cocoa, gelatin, dried coconut, and flavoring and coloring essences. Cooks swapped interesting recipes for sandwiches and cakes, and showed off skills at weekly "bring a plate" dances. Manufacturers issued recipe pamphlets which promoted their ingredients in "dainties" for polite morning and afternoon teas. The popular Lamington was cubes of cake coated in chocolate and coconut. The Pavlova—named after the ballerina Anna Pavlova and based on the New Zealand "meringue cake"—topped off the second stage in Australian cuisine, which was about to be transformed.

By the 1950s, food technologists had brought in the latest United States' know-how, which had been developed to feed Allied troops. This provided the technical, managerial and cultural foundation for the vertically integrated and generally foreign-owned agribusiness. At the same time, the wartime steelworks and munitions factories had been turned over to producing motor vehicles and refrigerators.

We need to appreciate the key role of private cars and refrigerators in the development of the supermarket. Until the 1950s, carters delivered much household food daily from door-to-door, or the housewives took their string bags to the corner store. Now, the car enabled the family to collect the shopping weekly from the more distant supermarket. Once home, milk and meat were now kept in the refrigerator.

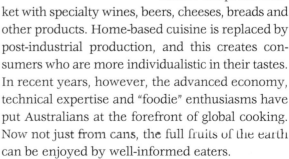

The food industry's goal was not only to grow and preserve food in sophisticated ways, but now also to cook it. The archetypal "convenience" dish, the TV dinner, was to be a complete meal frozen in a reheatable aluminum tray, although it was less successful than a range of dried Chinese meals, frozen pizzas, premixed cakes and Coca-Cola.

Restaurants and cafés grew in number and Australian families who had never dined out now took to well-priced and well-prepared Chinese meals; opinion-leaders hobnobbed in fashionable bistros. Since the 1960s, cookbooks have also proliferated and diversified.

This arrival of global cuisine has usually been attributed to Australia's strong post-war immigration program. Certainly, Australian society is now markedly multicultural. However, it had previously been a "mixing-pot" without accepting Italian, Chinese or other cooking. The latest culinary development is the "discovery" of Australia's indigenous ingredients.

Today, convenience products, fast food and restaurants threaten to replace domestic cooking in Australia, as in much of the developed world. A whole range of new artisan businesses tempt the market with specialty wines, beers, cheeses, breads and other products. Home-based cuisine is replaced by post-industrial production, and this creates consumers who are more individualistic in their tastes. In recent years, however, the advanced economy, technical expertise and "foodie" enthusiasms have put Australians at the forefront of global cooking. Now not just from cans, the full fruits of the earth can be enjoyed by well-informed eaters.

Eating out in restaurants and cafés is now very much part of the modern Australian lifestyle.

Native Australian Food

The rediscovery of ancient indigenous ingredients

by Andrew Fielke

Australia's newest cuisine paradoxically depends upon its oldest ingredients. When white settlers first arrived in Australia a little over two centuries ago, the country's Aborigines—who had inhabited the continent for some 40,000 years—had a remarkable understanding of its natural resources. However, it is in only in the last decade or so that the non-Aboriginal population of Australia has begun to discover its exciting range of indigenous food, not only obvious items such as kangaroo meat but a variety of wild seeds, nuts, fruit and vegetables known to the natives for thousands of years.

Aboriginal rock paintings in the Northern Territory show an emu and a lizard, both of which would have been roasted over a fire before being eaten.

Ironically, much of this ancient knowledge was in danger of being lost as many Aborigines left their traditional homelands and adopted new lifestyles.

The Aborigines' spiritual bonding with their land and their knowledge of its produce had been handed down from one generation to the next by their legends and stories. The first white settlers in Australia, noting that the natives were not agriculturalists in the accepted sense, dismissed them as simple hunters and gatherers. It has since been discovered that the Aborigines irrigated some areas of land, regulated the undergrowth and encouraged regrowth and genetic diversity by practicing controlled burning of the vegetation. Certain abundant food resources were actively managed and maintained. Seeds of fruits were often scattered after eating, and when eggs of the magpie goose were taken, a few nests were always left untouched. In South Australia, the Aborigines stored excess live fish from their catch in special traps.

Most foods were eaten raw, but some required special treatment such as roasting or pounding and leaching in running water to remove harmful toxins. Some foodstuffs were cooked, with witchetty grubs, kangaroos, smaller mammals, crabs, birds and fish being roasting over a fire. Wattle and Kurrajong seeds were roasted on red-hot coals, ground to a flour, mixed with water and baked to make a nutritious damper or seed cake.

The recent discovery of indigenous ingredients

by non-Aboriginal Australians was made possible largely by Vic Cherikoff, a research scientist at Sydney University, who was the first person to commence commercial collection and distribution of a range of native foods through his then fledgling company, Bush Tucker Supply Australia, in 1987. His company, and others like South Australia's Creative Native Australian Industries, distribute a wide range of native ingredients. From the handful of Australian chefs who initially took up the challenge of incorporating Australian native foods into modern and conventional recipes, there is now an ever-increasing acceptance of, and interest in, such ingredients.

A dragon lizard ready for the fire. A wide variety of seeds were also roasted on red-hot coals before being ground to make a nutritious flour.

The range of fruits, herbs, spices and nuts available has increased considerably, with responsible companies ensuring the sustainability of such wild foods through the practice of ecologically sound farming. Such companies also grow and market Australian native food plants for sale to commercial produce growers and home gardeners, and some also manufacture a range of gourmet food products made from the plants and fauna species. At the same time, there has been a proliferation of emu, yabby and barramundi farms.

Today's Australians have the unique good fortune to be able to use fruits, nuts, seeds, herbs, tubers, vegetables and animals just as they were some 40,000 years ago, unmanipulated by man through genetic engineering or selective breeding.

Restaurants like Adelaide's Red Ochre Grill are helping to introduce Australia's age-old bush foods to a wider audience, and the consistent success and international attention over the years demonstrates that the concept of a creative indigenous cuisine is far more than just a fad. Native foods are slowly but surely being integrated into Australian cuisine, although it is unlikely that large numbers of Australian restaurants will become dedicated "bush food" restaurants. Young Australian chefs now have the opportunity to use Australia's oldest ingredients to develop a fresh and innovative style of cuisine limited only by their imagination.

Mediterranean Influences

Australia moves from damper to focaccia

by Tess Mallos

One often-quoted statistic which reveals just how many immigrants from the Mediterranean have made Australia their home is that Melbourne has the third biggest population of people of Greek origin anywhere in the world, including Greece.

The immigration of hundreds of thousands of Mediterraneans—primarily Italians, Greeks and Lebanese—has had a profound impact on the cuisine of Australia, yet the changes in mainstream eating patterns happened only relatively recently.

As far back as the 1880s, small numbers of immigrants from Italy, Greece, Cyprus, Lebanon, Syria, Malta and Spain began arriving. In 1947, acknowledging the country's severe manpower shortage, the government decided that more immigrants were needed if Australia was to reach its full potential. By this time, only 2 percent of the population of 7.5 million was of non-Anglo-Celtic origin and the government continued targeting the British so that Australia's Anglo culture could be maintained.

But it was necessary to also include continental Europeans if Australia's population was to grow quickly. Displaced persons of Northern Europe and other Europeans were allowed, with large intakes from Latvia, Estonia, Lithuania, Poland, Holland, Germany, Austria, Czechoslovakia, Hungary, Romania, Yugoslavia, Italy, Greece and Malta. By 1991, almost 18 percent of the population—which had more than doubled to 16.5 million since 1947—did not speak English in the home. Today, Italians are the largest immigrant group after those from the UK and Ireland.

While Australia could provide the basic ingredients to allow these "New Australians" to maintain their dietary preferences, they were initially obliged to turn to their own gardens and to their own expertise in the kitchen. They made their own breads, yogurt, some cheeses, preserved meats and pasta, supplementing these with special foods imported by a few Italian, Greek and Lebanese stores.

Back in the 1940s, our "Greek" country garden provided us with the many vegetables and herbs not

A group of Italian Australians in Perth, Western Australia; Italians form the country's largest immigrant group after settlers from the United Kingdom and Ireland.

eaten by Australians of Anglo-Celtic background, as did the gardens of immigrant Italians and Lebanese. A number of Italians then set up market gardens to supply the many Italian-owned fruit and vegetable shops catering to the needs of the general public, as well as customers of Mediterranean background.

Because of the rapid increase in the numbers of immigrants arriving from the 1950s onwards, there was a greater opportunity to manufacture the foods they sought on a commercial scale, such as salamis, prosciutto, pepperoni and other preserved meats, Italian and Greek cheeses, yogurt, pasta and filo pastry. The ready availability of such products now made it possible for other Australians to become familiar with hitherto exotic foodstuffs.

Today, pizza and pasta are very much part of the Australian diet, as are Lebanese/Syrian tabouli and hommus, Greek tzatziki and taramosalata. There are olives galore, and sun-dried tomatoes became so popular in the mid 1980s that imports are now competing with Australian made products, along with sun-dried peppers. Italian and Greek breads (including the immensely popular focaccia) are now readily available—a vast change from the colonial bush bread or damper—and Lebanese pocket or pita breads are also firmly entrenched.

The majority of Australians in the past had an aversion to oil of any kind and the oiliness of Greek and Italian food was often criticized. The acceptance of olive oil began only when National Heart Foundation began urging Australians in the 1970s to replace some of their traditional butter, lard and drippings with polyunsaturated oils. Recent research has indicated that the incidence of heart disease is

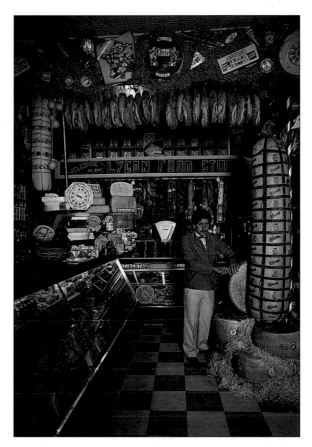

The large influx of immigrants from Mediterranean countries after WWII provided the impetus for the manufacture of a wide range of cheeses, processed meats, pasta and other products. This typical delicatessen is in Melbourne's Lygon Street.

lower among those following a "Mediterranean diet," with a high intake of complex carbohydrates (pasta, rice, bread and bulgur), vegetables and fruits, with more seafood than meat, plenty of legumes and olive oil, a monounsaturated oil.

Australians in the 1990s are the largest per capita consumers of olive oil outside the Mediterranean countries. This is a far cry from the 1940s, when the only olive oil in easy reach was in tiny bottles at the

That old British stalwart, roast lamb, is more likely to be enhanced with garlic and rosemary these days, thanks to the influence of Mediterranean cuisines.

In the early years of their culinary awakening, the first taste many Australians had of Mediterranean foods was during their "continental tours," when they had no option but to try salamis, pizzas, olives, strong cheeses, pasta or moussaka. Back home, with taste buds primed, they were more willing to accept the new foods gradually appearing in the market place. Food columnists were also responsible in the process of education, and when Australian-produced cookbooks began specializing in the cuisines of various countries because the basic foods were finally readily available and had gained acceptance, Australians could experiment with alacrity.

Finally, restaurants have always played a part. Australia was not a total culinary wilderness in the early days. There were Italian restaurants in Melbourne from the early 1920s, and in other areas there were many other restaurants featuring cuisines described as "Continental" and "French." These days, Italian restaurants abound, together with Greek and Lebanese/Syrian restaurants, while Spanish restaurants are increasing in popularity. Many restaurateurs, recognizing the suitability of Mediterranean food to Australia's climate and lifestyle, take the best of these foods which Australia now produces, combining them with skill and imagination and presenting their bill of fare as "Mediterranean-style."

pharmacy, its use confined to medicinal remedies and baby care.

Natural or "health food" stores catering principally to vegetarians were another factor in popularizing Mediterranean foods. Bulgur, the steamed crushed wheat of the Eastern Mediterranean, first became available to the general public through such outlets, as did yogurt, tahini, beans and, more recently, the couscous of Morocco.

The embarrassments of my youth—admitting to using olive oil on salads and vegetables, and eating "soured" milk (yogurt)—are unknown to my children and grandchildren; they can and do enjoy openly whatever they like in our culinarily enlightened society.

Australia's Asian Connection

Asian immigration has had a dramatic culinary impact

by Charmaine Solomon

From a culinary point of view, Australia is not the same country we migrated to 36 years ago, when we left the tropical island of Ceylon (now Sri Lanka) for Sydney—big, beautiful, bewildering. Forward scouts had warned us that Australia was a land where one could buy nothing in the way of "civilized" foods and that we should take our own supplies of spices.

Heeding the advice, I came armed with cans of curry powder my mother had blended for me. On the can was written, in her clear script, a basic recipe. With this as my lifeline, I was launched on the unknown waters of cooking real food for the first time. ("Real food" meaning meals to survive on, as distinct from the cakes and confectionery I had taken pleasure in creating.) There had been no need for me to prepare meals in Sri Lanka because every household had a resident cook. While there was a "sink or swim" feeling of being thrown in at the deep end, there was also a sense of real adventure.

This was the time of the White Australia policy. In order to obtain permission to settle in Australia, I had to provide proof of the requisite 75 percent of European blood. (Thankfully, my ancestors had arrived in Ceylon from Holland in the year 1714 and detailed genealogies of many Dutch families had been kept by the Dutch Burgher Union.) The cultural cringe was alive and well in Australia, but it was the newcomers who suffered from it. I learned to make spaghetti Bolognese and roasts almost before I learned to make a good curry.

When it came to grocery shopping, apart from the corner store with its basic supplies, there existed only the "Ham and Beef" shop, forerunner of today's delicatessen, but at that time the name was totally descriptive. There were also health food stores where one could purchase rice, split peas, curry powder and turmeric.

But what a difference the last three decades have made in the eating habits of Australians of Anglo-Celtic background, to whom the "baked dinner" was almost a religion, with services being held at least once a week; to whom a curry was what you did with the leftover roast and Chinese food the invention known as *chop suey*.

Now Australians delight in the opportunity of traveling through their taste buds, and often the journey takes them to Asia. *Yum cha (dim sum)* on weekends is becoming increasingly popular. If a Thai restaurant is known to be good, you had better book reservations. Indian restaurants are gaining popularity, especially those that offer regional or vegetarian food. Eat-in or take-away places specialize in noodles from Malaysia, *pho* from Vietnam, *laksa* from Singapore, satay and other quick meals that are incredibly tasty.

It's hard to believe that a generation ago, the average Aussie considered it the height of chic to visit the local Chinese restaurant. The sign outside assured the clientele that "Chinese and Australian" meals were served, and the menu was carefully vetted so that nothing too challenging confronted customers.

I think the change may have started with tourism to Asia. With their country placed in the Pacific, nearer to Asia than to Europe or America, vacations in Asia are more affordable to average Australians. Once travelers were exposed to the excellent, bargain-priced food, there was no going back. They came home to Australia keen to repeat their gastronomic experiences, even if it meant learning to cook the food themselves. They'd seen it tossed together in minutes at street stalls and felt it couldn't be too difficult—and it isn't.

In the 1960s, the emphasis was on Continental cuisines with their richness and long-cooking methods. It has now shifted to Asian cuisines with fresh flavors and the fast, healthy cooking styles of steaming and stir-frying. I am fortunate to have lived in Australia during decades of incredible change and had the opportunity to share my love of Asian cook-

Chinese prospectors who came to Australia during the 19th-century gold rushes were able to enjoy their own cuisine in private clubs and restaurants, as this illustration from a 1880 edition of The Australasian Sketcher *shows.*

ing through books and teaching. When referred to as the "mother of Asian cooking in Australia," I protest that I was only a midwife, merely easing its entry into this new area and sharing with others what I had to learn myself, how to cook Asian food in a Western country. I had a hard time convincing people that all Asian food did not have to be loaded with chilies. I learned not to wince when some earnest cook assured me that she made a "curry" with diced apples, bananas, sultanas and curry powder.

Chinese food was everything in a sweet and sour sauce, or deep-fried (including the ice-cream); Indonesian food was hot *sambals* which made tears run; Indian food was *pappadams* and cucumbers in yogurt and curries with no depth of flavor, no subtle fragrant spices but lots of cayenne powder. If not hot they were considered not "authentic," so one might say the public got what they deserved. As for Thai, Vietnamese, Cambodian, Laotian, Japanese, Nonya, Burmese, Korean cuisines—the palette of flavors that now enrapturing many Australians—they were not even blips on the horizon.

In the 1960s, I used to write to my family in Sri Lanka for stocks of spices. In the 1970s, Asian ingredients started to become more accessible, mainly in the Chinatown areas of capital cities. In the 1980s, because of the influx of Asian immigrants and refugees, there was a quantum leap in growing and distributing numerous Asian herbs, vegetables and fruits. Chili sauces and other flavorings began to be produced locally. Now, in this country with its Western heritage, one is able to purchase almost as wide a range of Asian ingredients as in Asia itself.

Looking back over 25 years of food writing, I can see from my early books that at first there was no choice but to use dried curry leaves, lemongrass and galangal, and explain to readers how to make coconut milk since a quality product was not available in cans. Now, while some remote country towns might still be reliant on dried herbs, it is most unlikely that the supermarket does not carry at least a couple of brands of canned coconut milk.

As for big cities, every suburban shopping center has an Asian supermarket, perhaps more than one. The aisles buzz with activity, especially on weekends. The customers are not all Asian either. Young chefs who are not afraid of blazing trails are making a mockery of the well known lines penned by Rudyard Kipling, "East is East and West is West and never the twain shall meet." In the capable hands of today's high-profile chefs, ingredients and cooking methods of both East and West are meeting and merging. The result is an exciting blend in which neither one predominates, but each enhances the other.

Australia is emerging from the shadow of "the old country," finding its place in the Asia-Pacific region and realizing that the cuisines of its Asian neighbors are more relevant to its climate than those of Europe. The great land extending from the tropics to the south allows Australians to enjoy the gamut from mangoes, rambutans, kaffir limes, pandan leaves, crabs of dinner-plate size, to Atlantic salmon and ocean trout from the icy waters off Tasmania.

There is an exploration taking place, a happy discovery of new ingredients and fresh flavors. East and West are not only meeting, they are embracing. The coating of chopped *konbu* (sea kelp) on the rare slice of ocean trout, the Indian *tandoori* marinade on a char-grilled kangaroo fillet, the snow peas and fresh water chestnut in the salad, the threads of Thai lime leaf and slivers of lemongrass in a tomato broth, the hint of galangal in the crab-filled ravioli perhaps give us proof of an emerging uniquely Australian cuisine.

Asian vegetables are now eagerly sought by Australians of all ethnic backgrounds

The Great Aussie Barbie

Alfresco dining is a national institution

by Tony Baker

Australia stands alone among the nations of the world in having launched a tourism boom with a barbecue. Back in 1983, actor Paul Hogan appeared in TV commercials designed to entice Americans to Australia, which wound up with him at a barbecue saying in his familiar Aussie drawl "C'mon. C'mon 'n' say g'day. I'll slip an extra shrimp on the barbie." It was stupendously successful because it captured the easygoing hedonism of the sunburnt country.

Australians have made an art form of eating outdoors. It is rare to find an Australian house without a barbecue, and even a city apartment is likely to have one on the balcony. The main roads, parks, beaches and picnic areas have public barbecue facilities. When the eating out boom began in the 1970s, among its earliest manifestations were pubs with beer gardens where customers bought and cooked their own steaks with salads and sauces on an adjacent buffet. When two Australian men stop talking about sport, there is a good chance they are busy swapping their secret recipes for the perfect marinade.

*Right &
Opposite*:
*The traditional
bush camp, a
necessity for
drovers and
travelers in the
early days, is
now included in
tour operators'
packages in parts
of Australia.*

There is, though, much more to Australians' love affair with their great outdoors. It can be said that before the evolution of today's creative cuisine, there was a much earlier indigenous style known as "bush tucker," built around a billy can on an open fire or, more recently, a camp oven. Today's new wave chefs make ingenious and appetizing use of Australia's unique flora and fauna, but they are only following on the inventiveness or necessity of those hardy 19th-century shearers, drovers and diggers who learned how to cook kangaroo, quandongs (wild peaches), emu, wild goat and even camel in basic conditions. These were eaten with damper, a simple bread of flour, water, milk or beer with butter and oil, perhaps flavored with native herbs and cooked in a billy or bush oven on an open fire. Today's chic city restaurants often serve a sophisticated version of damper to an appreciative clientele. Bush tucker has been refined in a most glamorous way in the Red Centre, beneath the

MacDonnell Ranges outside Alice Springs, where restaurateur Ron Tremaine provides billy tea, damper, bush salad and Territory beef served under the stars—an experience not to be forgotten. I think the original Australian joke is the bushman's recipe for cooking cockatoo. Catch a cockatoo and boil it with two stones. When the stones are soft, the bird is ready. Another version commands you to throw away the cockatoo and eat the stones. Another bush recipe calls for 3 medium-sized camels, 700 bushels of vegetables, 1,000 gallons of gravy and 2 small rabbits. You are directed to spend several months preparing and simmering the stew, which will serve 3,800; if more people are expected, add the 2 rabbits.

The final touch to any Aussie barbecue is a handful of gum leaves in the fire for that dinky di (authentic) outback flavor.

Thanks to its climate, eating out around Australia is also a mass affair. Rare is the Australian event, from the running of the Melbourne Cup to the Adelaide arts festival, which does not feature outdoor eating, usually around a "barbie," perhaps a picnic or that sturdy Australian staple, meat pie with tomato sauce.

When Victoria embarked on a tourism promotion campaign, the promoters did so with the world's longest lunch at which hundreds of people sat down to seafood on a long pier. There are now at least a dozen regional wine and food festivals in which premier restaurants set up in wine cellar doors for a day or weekend and people travel the district for a glass of wine and plate of food at each.

Despite the national passion for the outdoors, it is only in recent years that what seems the most obvious way of enjoying this has caught on. Australia's liquor licensing laws and local council regulations once made pavement or boulevard eating and drinking impossible. Battle was joined and won and today, entire city streets from Fremantle in Western Australia to the tourist belts of Queensland are now lined with tables and chairs. That alfresco feeling is also an integral part of many frontline restaurants. Where once the backyard was the place for the empties, today it is likely to be a shaded garden with foodies taking their ease. When making a booking at an Australian restaurant, it's wise to check the weather forecast and then inquire whether there is an outdoor option.

The national partiality for eating outdoors has perhaps also contributed to Australians' longevity. From bush tucker to barbies, Australians have learned the simple pleasures of the plain grill and taught themselves to be inventive when devising salads. Paul Hogan's shrimp on the barbie was a health as well as a lifestyle statement.

Gourmet Dining in the Country

The transformation of the Australian countryside

by Marieke Brugman

Only a generation ago, the prospect of a handsome dining room, a fine meal and superb wines away from an Australian metropolis would have been merely fanciful, unless one had the good fortune to be visiting a traditional farming family. In less than twenty years, there has been a virtual revolution across the countryside, both in terms of the variety of choices of character-rich places to stay overnight and to eat regionally focused cuisine, and in terms of the agricultural landscape itself.

Long anchored in largely Anglo-Celtic traditions, the rural landscape was dominated by sheep, cattle and wheat. The farms (known as stations) supported the extended families of the rural "gentry" as well as their workers and families, and because of their isolation, were virtually self-sufficient.

The enclave of buildings would have included a schoolhouse, stables, shearing sheds, outlying buildings for machinery and repairs, and a meathouse in which to hang home-killed carcasses. Meat, because of its bountifulness, tended to form the major dietary staple. Rabbit and wild duck in season were shot for the table, poultry raised, the house cow milked, an orchard kept and a vegetable garden tended. Bulk dry-foods would be procured on long, infrequent forays to the nearest "town."

Homestead kitchens were the norm and the hub of social life. Huge wood-burning stoves allowed the preparation of copious quantities of food. A secondary kitchen or separate space was devoted to the processing and preserving of jams, pickles, chutneys and sauces. Often there was a stone-lined cellar beneath for the storage of orderly rows of preserving jars with their aesthetic placements of fruit and vegetables. Roast dinners were typical of fare which could be characterized as plain, simple, hearty, honest cooking with "fancy" cooking reserved for the dessert repertoire.

Much of this is now a thing of the past, yet never before have the gastronomic opportunities in country Australia been more bright. The increasingly adventurous and curious nature of the Australian

One of the many hundreds of delicious options throughout the Australian countryside, the Uraidla Aristologist in the Adelaide hills offers excellent cuisine.

Country-fresh produce can be enjoyed in restaurants, cafés, country homes or simply on a picnic.

variations on steak and chips or a mixed grill), Victoria's spectacularly scenic Great Ocean Road is now known as "the cappuccino coast," testament to a myriad of cafés serving proper coffee, lovely wines, and everything from focaccia and pasta to fresh salads and local grilled fish.

Along with dynamic changes in agriculture—partly the result of leading chefs encouraging producers and growers to diversify—so too the countryside is reinventing itself. One of the earliest examples of a new rural identity was the pioneering Howqua Dale Gourmet Retreat, founded in 1977 in the glorious sub-alpine region of north-eastern Victoria. Howqua Dale was one of the first properties in Australia to take advantage of its beautiful location and to

palate has not confined itself to city sophistication. From the 1950s, when Australians started to enjoy a somewhat Westernized rendition of Chinese food, they have consistently expanded their repertoire of flavors, so that now even ordinary households all over the country include ginger, garlic, cilantro and basil in their weekly shopping lists.

Where once the dining options outside major cities were limited to a counter-meal at a pub (basic

offer city guests a unique combination of an authentic bush environment with a highly refined sense of Australian hospitality, luxurious accommodation, soothing views and superb food with excellent wines from a mostly Australian cellar. The cuisine is proudly Australian and draws for its inspiration on what is locally available during the season: herbs and vegetables from the garden, wild mushrooms gathered from nearby fields and forests, chestnuts, walnuts, honey and berries from neighboring farms, wine from the next valley at Delatite, venison and salmon from the Yarra Valley and eggs from free-roving "chooks."

There are now hundreds of opportunities for city residents and overseas visitors to explore an intricate tapestry of establishments flung far and wide, which are testament to Australia as a paradise for food and wine lovers.

One of the newest but most remote properties, Haggerstone Island in Far North Queensland, gives a unique experience to the tiny number of visitors it takes at any one time. Totally self-sufficient in its tropical environment where an abundance of fish virtually jump out of the water, each day's meals rely entirely on what has been picked, netted, speared or caught that day. Coral trout, sardines, coconuts, exotic fruits and hot-climate vegetables, so extraordinarily fresh they need little adornment, remind urbanites of the rare experience of enjoying the wonderful flavors and texture of ingredients which are still "alive." And the vacation is much enhanced for guests because they participate in the daily harvest and preparation of communal meals.

It is doubtful that Australia has or will develop distinctively regional cuisines, partly because chefs are spoiled by their easy access to such a huge variety of ingredients. However, chefs such as Maggie Beer (whose Pheasant Farm in South Australia gave a new meaning to regional food) demonstrated the value of cooking so close to the source. She was responsible for creating significant dishes which celebrated a region's specialties, and also subtly commented on their particular rural culture and the importance of "natural" and unadulterated food.

These attitudes continue to exert a widespread influence over the practices of country cooks. Kate Lamont, one of the rising young stars in Western Australia, has created a cuisine at her family's winery in the Swan Valley that is based on those ingredients most readily available to her. These include outstanding goat cheese made by one of Australia's leading cheesemakers, Gay Kervella, who runs her organically managed farm on a remote and beautiful peak in the next valley surrounded by national park; marron (freshwater crayfish) farmed in ponds up the road; olive oil and sourdough bread produced at an old monastery in New Norcia; and vegetables and fruit from neighbors.

Many of Australia's wine regions have become the hub for a new form of country culture. A number of wineries have created their own restaurants and cooks are establishing their businesses in wine-growing locales, with the emphasis on country fresh foods and highlighting of regional wines. From grand and luxurious to simple, rustic old homesteads, elaborately decorated country pubs, wonderful manor houses and picturesque stone cottages have been brought back to life. Redolent of a bygone era and encapsulating the spirit of a region, they offer modern comfort in individualistic settings.

The Australian countryside is becoming a haven for food cognoscenti, especially for travelers curious to experience a way of life that harks back to some old-fashioned values in terms of friendship and generosity, but which is also touched by the modern influences of the multi-ethnic, eclectic society that makes Australian cities exciting.

A New World of Wine

A peaceful revolution that everyone can celebrate

by Tony Baker

Despite Australia's reputation as a nation of beer drinkers, on any day there are more than 10,000 wines on sale around the country. What is most remarkable is that almost all of them will be somewhere between good and majestic.

The Australian wine story goes back as far as the modern nation itself, with grapevines being part of the cargo of the First Fleet which landed at Sydney Cove in 1788. Wine was in commercial production in Sydney and Tasmania by the 1820s. Today, some 750 wineries spread across every state and territory, although South Australia, New South Wales, Victoria and Western Australia have the principal regions. South Australia can lay claim to being Australia's wine state, producing six out of ten glasses of the national vintage.

Australia has always exported wine. In the peak years up to World War II, more was sent abroad than consumed at home. But in the past generation there has been a revolution in Australian winemaking. Australian winemakers have applied modern technology to the ancient mixture of art and craft involved in transforming ripe grapes into drinks of infinite complexity. This has resulted in the surge in popularity at home and the increasing demand abroad, where Australian wines now rank among the best of what are known as New World wines.

Until this revolution took hold, the typical Australian wine was fortified: sherry, port, muscat and so on. Today, it is a red or white table wine, usually with an attractive label, fully and accurately detailing what grape varieties were used, where they were grown and, often, who made it. Some winemakers have even achieved the superstar status accorded to great French chefs and approaching that of rock musicians.

Australian winemakers still use some generic terms on their labels, which broadly indicate the style of wine or some supposed European affinity, such as port, sherry, burgundy and chablis. This tradition is rapidly disappearing in favor of varietal descriptions showing the particular grape variety or blend such as riesling, chardonnay, shiraz, cabernet sauvignon or cabernet shiraz, denoting a blend of those two red grapes.

The change to varietal labeling is partly the result of an agreement with the European Union and also attributable to Australian pride and confidence its products can truly stand alone. It has been said that describing wine is about as easy as weighing music, but in essence the reason why Australian wines are so good and so keenly sought after is that they are fresh, clean and bursting with the gamut of grape flavors.

Opposite:
One of the country's top winemakers, Wolf Blass, contemplates a glass of South Australian wine.

Part Two: Chefs, Ingredients & Recipes
The Chefs of Australia
by Rita Erlich

What exactly is Australian cooking? It's open-minded, it's skilled, it's not weighted down by tradition and, as a profession, it attracts some of the best minds in the country. Australia is where some of the finest chefs have had no formal culinary training, and where the proportion of great women cooks is much higher than anywhere else.

There are in fact two aspects of Australian food. The first is the ingredients, all those distinctively Australian items such as kangaroo and emu and bush tomatoes and bunya nuts. But there's also Australian food in terms of how ingredients are cooked and served by Australians. It is this second aspect of food that makes eating in Australia so rewarding, and as the following recipes show, it is the striking amalgam of styles and ingredients that distinguishes Australian cooks.

You can never be sure what you'll eat next. It might be a savory pumpkin risotto cake with smoked kangaroo as Bethany Finn of the Adelaide Hilton makes it. It might be a chicken breast on couscous mixed with pomegranate seeds and served with pistachio butter as prepared by Andrew Blake. It could be a mousse of snapper and shrimp wrapped in a *nori* omelet created by Christine Manfield. It might be Marieke Brugman's classic pavlova, a meringue dessert regarded as an Australian classic, or a cheesecake made from native Illawarra plums as prepared by Guido van Baelen of the Sydney Airport Hilton.

Most modern cooking, whatever the country, now has an international flavor. To some extent, fine cooking has always been international, and it has been the strength of the Hilton hotel chain that it provided fine dining restaurants where the quality of cooking and excellence of service were hallmarks. In the late 60s and 70s, when grand restaurants were few, the Hilton dining rooms were standard bearers and important training grounds for cooks and waiters.

The formality and hierarchy of international hotel kitchens is often different from the easier structure of Australian restaurant kitchens, but there is a fruitful exchange of dialogue between the two styles. The Hilton now often showcases Australian chefs in the way that French chefs used to appear for limited seasons. The Melbourne Hilton, for example, invited three top Australian chefs (including Paul Merrony and Cheong Liew, who have contributed to this book) to limited seasons in the prestigious Cliveden Room Restaurant. Herbert Franceschini at the Brisbane Hilton launched an on-going guest chef program which has honored Australian chefs.

Opposite:
Typical of the new breed of innovative young chefs, Andrew Blake is always on the move.

Australia's top chefs have played their part in encouraging growers and suppliers. Australia has a remarkably fine range of produce and a growing number of specialized producers who are able to continue and even flourish because of a network of enterprising and dedicated chefs. One chef might find a specialist producing corn-fed chickens or exquisite baby beans, or a supplier of Illawarra plums or bush tomatoes, but everyone will soon know about them. It is not unknown for chefs to telephone one another for information: "Where did you get your squab?" "What's your source for warrigal greens?" Stephanie Alexander is particularly good at tracking down ingredients and suppliers, and her book, *Stephanie's Australia*, is a comprehensive guide to the best Australian food and its producers.

There's a new kind of internationalism in cooking now. The United States has been particularly innovative with a range of mixed cuisines. English-speaking countries, Australia included, are going through an East-meets-West phase, as indeed are many Asian countries. One reason for the international flavors is that chefs and restaurateurs travel. They all see the same new books and magazines and study the same photographs. What is hot in New York one week will soon appear on tables in London, Melbourne and Sydney.

But Australia's food internationalism is slightly different. Australia is an immigrant country, with each successive wave of immigration bringing its own food and flavors. Consider the origins of many of the chefs who have contributed to this book. Cheong Liew came from Malaysia, Marieke Brugman's parents were born in Holland, Alla Wolf-Tasker was born in Vienna of Russian parents, Dietmar Sawyere's father was Swiss, Beh Kim Un is Malaysian-born, Bill Marchetti's parents were Italian and German, Tetsuya Wakuda is Japanese.

What makes the immigrant tradition so special is that all those disparate backgrounds and cooking traditions have blended into a multicultural mainstream. Consider what the Australian-born chefs do: Christine Manfield offers a tea-smoked yellowfin tuna with a sweet and sour fennel salad; Stephanie Alexander uses Moroccan-inspired preserved lemon with Tasmanian salmon; Bethany Finn seasons roast lamb with Middle-Eastern *harissa* and accompanies it by Indian chick-pea curry and *naan* bread. In the kitchen, everyone is multilingual.

A surprising proportion of Australia's top chefs began their careers in other fields. They are not chefs in the European tradition, people who trained in the industry from a tender age. Their experiences before turning to restaurants inform their views of food and cooking, and are perhaps responsible for their open-minded approach.

Their recipes keep developing. For example, Paul Merrony's salad of turnips and roast tomatoes began as a simple salad of roast tomatoes, a minimalist dish that was a revelation at a time when the number of ingredients and garnishes on the plate was meant to be an index of quality. It has been modified over the years, another point of difference with European chefs whose dishes may remain unchanged for twenty years.

The recipes in this book represent a cross section of the best Australian contemporary cuisine. In short, these are the tastes of Australia.

Australian Ingredients

Australian cuisine draws on ingredients
from around the world

BASIL, THAI: The most commonly used Thai basil in Australia is *horapa*; it has a distinct fragrance but European sweet basil can be substituted.

BLACK MUSTARD SEEDS: Used in Indian-influenced dishes; do not substitute yellow mustard seeds.

BLACK ONION SEEDS: Sometimes known as nigella, these seeds (called *kalonji* in India) should be available in Indian stores; black sesame seeds could be substituted.

BUNYA NUTS: Starchy nuts from the cone of the bunya pine native to Australia. They are similar in taste and texture to chestnuts, although each bunya nut contains about five times as much meat as a chestnut.

BUSH TOMATOES: Sometimes known as desert raisins, these small intensely flavored berries grow on a native shrub related to the tomato. Substitute sun-dried tomatoes.

CHILIES: The most commonly used chilies are finger-length red or green fresh chilies and the tiny, much hotter bird's-eye chilies.

CILANTRO: Fresh coriander leaves, known in some countries as cilantro, are popular in many dishes with a Southeast Asian inspiration. The roots are also used in Thai cuisine. Any Asian store or market and many regular supermarkets and vegetable shops sell cilantro or fresh coriander leaf.

CLOUD EAR FUNGUS: Also known as wood fungus, this is a shriveled greyish-brown

Basil

Native Australian products can be purchased in a number of specialty shops in major Australian cities and can also be ordered directly from.

Australian Native Produce Industries
P.O. Box 163
Paringa
South Australia 5340
Australia

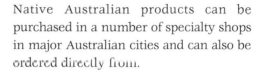

Bunya Nuts

Bush Tucker Supply Australia
P.O. Box B103
Boronia Park
New South Wales 2111
Australia

Bush Tomatoes

Illawarra Plums

Kaffir Lime Leaf

Lemon Aspen

Lemon Myrtle Leaves

fungus that swells to at least four times its original size after soaking in warm water for 10–15 minutes.

COUSCOUS: Semolina grains popular in Middle Eastern cooking, sold in packets and generally pre-cooked.

CRÈME FRAÎCHE: A slightly soured thick cream used in French cooking; look for it in supermarkets or combine thick cream with a little plain yogurt.

FISH SAUCE: A pungent salty sauce used in Thai and Vietnamese cuisine.

GALANGAL: A rhizome that is a member of the ginger family, galangal is widely used in Southeast Asian cuisine and should be available fresh in any Asian market. Alternatively, jars of water-packed galangal exported from Thailand can be used as a substitute.

HIJIKI: Japanese seaweed, generally available dried; soak in warm water until swollen.

ILLAWARRA PLUMS: Dark red berries from the native Brown Pine, these have a rich berry flavor. Any small purple or red plums can be substituted.

JAPANESE HORSERADISH: Widely referred to by its Japanese name, *wasabi*, this comes from a root that is not a true horseradish, although it shares the same nose-tingling properties. Although sold ready-mixed in tubes, it is preferable to buy cans of *wasabi*

powder and mix to a paste with water shortly before using.

KAFFIR LIME LEAF: The intensely fragrant leaf of the kaffir or leprous lime tree is used in Southeast Asian, particularly Thai, dishes. Available fresh in specialty shops.

LAVER: A seaweed widely used in Japanese cuisine and known as *nori*, this is sold in packets and is normally toasted and crisp. If it has gone soggy, hold over a flame for a few seconds to regain its crispness. *Nori* is also sold seasoned and eaten as a snack.

LEMON ASPEN: These small pale lemon-colored fruits which are native to the tropical regions of Australia have a sharp citrus flavor. Use lemon juice as a substitute.

LEMON GRASS: A lemon-scented grass found throughout Southeast Asia and now grown in warmer areas of Australia, this looks like a miniature leek. Use only the bottom 4 inches of the stalk. Available in most Asian stores and markets.

LEMON MYRTLE LEAVES: Similar in fragrance to lemon verbena, these come from a native rainforest tree; kaffir lime leaves make a good substitute.

MACADAMIA NUT: An Australian native also known as the Queensland bush nut, this was popularized by American growers in Hawaii.

MARRON: A freshwater crayfish native to Australia, this expensive delicacy is now being pond-reared. Any other crustacean such as yabby (see below), flathead lobster or slipper lobster (known in Australia as Moreton Bay or Balmain bugs) can be used as a substitute.

MIRIN: A sweet Japanese rice wine used only in cooking. Keeps indefinitely.

MORETON BAY BUGS: This is the Queensland term for the slipper or flathead lobster, *Thenus orientalis,* found throughout the Indo-Pacific region.

PALM SUGAR: Used in Southeast Asian cooking, this is made from the sap of the inflorescences of the aren or coconut palm. If not available, substitute soft brown sugar with a touch of maple syrup.

POLENTA: A fine cornmeal popular in Italy, this is usually boiled and allowed to cool into firm cakes, which are then fried or grilled. Sold in any specialty store and many supermarkets.

SAKE: Japanese rice wine, which keeps up to one month after opening; if unavailable, substitute Chinese rice wine for cooking.

SHALLOT: Small clusters of what look like miniature onions with brownish or purplish skin, these are sweeter and less watery than regular onions. Sometimes known in Australia as eshallots or eschallots, these must not be confused with spring onions, widely and incorrectly called shallots in Australia.

SHRIMP PASTE, DRIED: A pungent seasoning used throughout Southeast Asia, this should be available in any Asian store.

SICHUAN PEPPER: The reddish brown berry of the prickly ash or fagara tree, used primarily in Sichuan Chinese cuisine.

STAR ANISE: This Chinese spice resembles a flower with eight petals, each containing a shiny brown seeds. Has a pronounced aniseed flavor.

TAMARILLO: An egg-shaped fruit with a dark red skin and orangey-red flesh with edible seeds. The tamarillo has an acid flavor and unique fragrance. No real substitute.

TURMERIC: Fresh turmeric is used in some Southeast Asian dishes and is available in many Australian markets; if this is not available, substitute 1 teaspoon of powdered turmeric for 1 inch fresh turmeric.

WAKAME: A very popular seaweed in Japan, this is sold either dried or salted. Soak to soften before using. *Wakame* does not need cooking.

WARRIGAL GREENS: Known botanically as *Tetragonia,* this is a fleshy green-leafed plant native to Australia and New Zealand. Substitute English spinach.

YABBY: A freshwater crustacean often found or reared in dams in Australia, this can be substituted by any crayfish or marine lobster.

Palm Sugar

Shallots

Warrigal Greens

Yabby

PUMPKIN RISOTTO CAKES WITH SMOKED KANGAROO

Bethany Finn, The Grange Brasserie, Adelaide Hilton

This imaginative recipe of pumpkin with Italian rice fashioned into savory cakes makes an excellent start to a meal.

$^3/_4$ **pound pie pumpkin or winter squash**
$^3/_4$ **cup olive oil**
salt and pepper to taste
1 onion, finely diced
6 cloves garlic, finely chopped
2 bay leaves
1 cup Arborio or other Italian rice
1–1$^1/_2$ cups hot chicken stock
1$^1/_4$ cups grated Parmesan cheese
$^1/_2$ cup white flour
1 egg
$^1/_2$ cup milk
3 cups fresh bread crumbs
4 tablespoons butter
5 ounces smoked kangaroo, beef or lamb, sliced
10 deep-fried sage leaves, optional

Opposite:
Salt and pepper shakers from Ventura Design, Lilyfield, Sydney; cutlery from Villeroy & Boch, French's Forest, Sydney.

Cut the pumpkin piece in half. Rub one half with a little olive oil and roast in a 325°F oven for 30-45 minutes, until soft. Scrape the flesh away from the skin and pass the flesh through a fine sieve. Season with salt and pepper to taste.

Peel the remaining pumpkin and cut the flesh into $^1/_4$-inch dice. Steam for a few minutes until half-cooked, then set aside.

Heat the oil in a wide saucepan and sauté the onion until transparent. Add the garlic and bay leaves, stir for a few seconds, then add the rice and sauté until the rice is thoroughly coated with oil. Turn the heat down to the absolute minimum and pour in 1 cup of hot chicken stock. Stir well and cover the rice with waxed paper. Set the rice aside for 7 minutes, then stir in the diced steamed pumpkin. Cover the rice again and leave for another 7 minutes to absorb the stock and expand. If the rice seems too dry, add a little more of the chicken stock and set aside. The amount of liquid needed depends to some extent on the age of the rice. The rice should have a chewy texture when cooked; it should not be crunchy or soggy.

Remove the cooked rice from the heat, stir in the Parmesan cheese and season with salt and pepper to taste. Spread on a tray to cool, then refrigerate.

Shortly before you wish to serve the risotto cakes, remove the rice mixture from the refrigerator. Shape into 10 balls, dust with flour, dip in the egg beaten with milk and coat with bread crumbs. Pat each end of the balls to flatten slightly. Heat the butter and fry the risotto cakes until golden brown on both sides. Serve immediately, garnishing each with a slice of smoked kangaroo and a teaspoonful of the reserved pumpkin purée. Garnish with deep-fried sage leaves if desired.

OYSTER CAPPUCCINO

Damien Pignolet, Bistro Moncur, Sydney

A superbly concentrated soup of oysters and mussel juice topped with whipped cream flavored with a hint of the soup, this is served in a cup just like Australia's favorite form of coffee, cappuccino. Although it may be extravagant to prepare, the result is so sublime for those who love oysters that it's well worth while. If you do not want to open the oysters yourself and have an obliging fishmonger, make sure he reserves the juice that comes out of them as you will need it. Serves 6.

4 pounds mussels in the shell
$\frac{1}{2}$ cup dry white wine
$\frac{1}{2}$ cup short-grain rice
$2\frac{1}{2}$ cups chicken stock
5 ounces fresh button mushrooms, caps and
    stalks chopped
60 oysters in the shell
$2\frac{1}{2}$ cups *crème fraîche*
freshly ground black pepper to taste
juice of 2 lemons
10 tablespoons whipping cream

Clean the mussels and put in a large pan with the wine. Cover and cook until the mussels open. Strain the mussel juice through a cheesecloth or muslin and add sufficient water to make $2\frac{1}{2}$ cups. Put the liquid into a clean saucepan, reserving the mussels for some other dish.

Add the rice and chicken stock to the saucepan, bring to a boil, cover and simmer until the rice is soft. Add the mushrooms and cook for another 10 minutes. Transfer to a blender and purée.

Open the oysters, taking care to keep the juices. Set 12 oysters aside as a garnish and blend the remainder with about $\frac{1}{4}$ cup of the puréed rice and mushroom mixture. Pass through a fine sieve into the balance of the purée. Remove $\frac{1}{2}$ cup of the purée and reserve.

Put the remaining purée in a pan and heat, working in the *crème fraîche*. Take care not to let the mixture boil. Adjust the seasoning with pepper and lemon juice; salt should not be necessary because of the saltiness of the mussel liquid.

Whip the cream stiffly and flavor it to taste with some or all of the reserved $\frac{1}{2}$ cup of purée. Divide the soup among six deep soup bowls, add two raw oysters per serving, top with a large spoonful of the whipped cream and grind some black pepper on top. Serve immediately.

YABBY AND ASPARAGUS SOUFFLÉ

Gerda Eilts, The Garden Restaurant, Parmelia Perth Hilton

A basic soufflé is lifted out of the ordinary with the inclusion of yabbies and asparagus. The baked soufflés are reheated in a cream sauce scented with tarragon and Parmesan cheese. Serves 6.

 18 raw yabbies or 18 medium-sized shrimp, still in the shell
 1 pound green asparagus
 5 tablespoons butter
 10 tablespoons white flour
 $\frac{1}{2}$ cup chicken stock
 $\frac{1}{2}$ cup milk
 salt and pepper to taste
 freshly grated nutmeg to taste
 4 egg yolks, lightly beaten
 6 egg whites
 10 tablespoons cream
 1 heaped tablespoon chopped fresh tarragon
 6 ounces gruyère cheese, grated (about $1^{1}/_{2}$ cups)

Opposite:
Plate by Alessi
from Ventura
Design, Lilyfield,
Sydney.

Bring a saucepan of lightly salted water to a boil. Add the yabbies or shrimp, return the water to a boil and immediately remove the pan from the heat. Stand for 5 minutes before removing the seafood. Drain the yabbies or shrimp, peel, cut in half lengthwise and remove the intestinal tract. Set the yabby or shrimp halves aside and discard the shells.

Blanch the asparagus in lightly salted boiling water for 2 minutes, then drain. Cut and reserve the tips and cut the remaining asparagus pieces into $\frac{1}{2}$-inch pieces.

Melt the butter and add the flour, stirring gently for 2–3 minutes. Slowly add the chicken stock and milk and cook over very low heat for 10 minutes, stirring from time to time. Add salt, pepper and nutmeg to taste, then fold in the egg yolks. Add the asparagus pieces, reserving the tips.

Beat the egg whites stiffly and then fold a couple of spoonfuls into the sauce. Carefully fold in the remaining egg whites.

Lightly grease 6 ramekins or individual soufflé dishes with butter, then put 4 yabby or shrimp halves into each. Fill each ramekin with the egg mixture. Stand the ramekins in a baking dish half-filled with water and bake in a 350°F oven for 20–25 minutes. Cool, unmold and set aside. The soufflés can be prepared several hours in advance.

Just before the soufflés are required, put each into a heat-proof bowl and pour over some of the cream. Put 2 of the reserved yabby or shrimp halves on top and scatter with a little fresh tarragon. Add gruyère cheese and bake at 350°F for 8 minutes. Serve immediately, garnished with the reserved asparagus spears.

TERRINE OF RABBIT WITH PRUNES

Damien Pignolet, Bistro Moncur, Sydney

2 wild rabbits with livers or 1 farmed rabbit,
   about 3 pounds
2 tablespoons Armagnac or Cognac
1 teaspoon coarsely ground black pepper
3 teaspoons fresh thyme leaves
¾ pound pork shoulder
¾ pound pork back fat
1 teaspoon oil
1 small onion, finely diced
1 large clove garlic, chopped
1 teaspoon *Quatre Épices* (page 134)
2 tablespoons white wine
1 bay leaf
1 egg
2 tablespoons finely chopped parsley
12–14 prunes, stones removed
rabbit stock (page 134)

Remove all the flesh from the rabbits, reserving one of the loin fillets in one piece. Put the fillet in a dish and moisten with a little of the Armagnac, some of the pepper and a pinch of the thyme leaves. Cover and chill. Reserve the rabbit livers. Use the bones to make the stock (page 134).

Dice the rabbit meat, pork shoulder and pork fat roughly. Heat the oil in a small pan and sauté the diced onion until it turns transparent. Add the garlic, remaining pepper, thyme and *quatre épices.* Add the white wine, remaining Armagnac and bay leaf. Mix well, cover and chill for 4 hours.

Transfer the mixture to a bowl. Add the egg, chopped parsley, chopped reserved rabbit livers and some salt to taste. Beat well until firm.

Grease a terrine with a little softened butter. Put in one-quarter of the minced mixture and press the top down firmly with the back of a spoon. Put a layer of half the prunes down the center of this and top with another quarter of the mixture, pressing down firmly. Lay the rabbit fillet on the center of this and add another quarter of the mixture. Put the remaining prunes over the top, add the final portion of rabbit and pork mixture and press the top. Tap the terrine firmly on the top of the bench, cover and refrigerate for 1 hour.

Put the terrine in a baking dish with hot water halfway up the sides of the terrine. Bake at 350°F for 30 minutes, then carefully pour off most of the fat. Pour in some or all of the stock to cover the meat. Cover and return the terrine to the oven for another 30–60 minutes. The terrine is cooked when the fatty liquids look clear and the mixture has begun to pull away from the sides. Remove from the oven and place a weight on top. Leave until cold, then remove the weight and refrigerate the terrine for at least 3 days before serving. If the top is sealed with melted pork fat, it will keep refrigerated for up to 2 weeks.

OYSTERS WITH LIME AND LEMON GRASS DRESSING

Beh Kim Un, Monsoon and Isthmus of Kra, Melbourne

One of the most popular appetizers from the Monsoon and Isthmus of Kra restaurants in Melbourne, this recipe provides enough for 3 oysters per serving. However, as they are usually so enthusiastically received, you may wish to double the amounts to allow for 6 oysters each.

12 fresh oysters in the shell
1 cup spinach leaves
$^{1}/_{2}$ cup button mushrooms
sliced red chili to garnish (optional)

Lime and Lemon grass Dressing:

scant 3 tablespoons chopped palm sugar
** (preferably coconut)**
$^{1}/_{2}$ cup lime or lemon juice
3 whole cilantro plants
1 clove garlic, very finely minced
1 stalk lemon grass, bottom 3 inches only,
** finely sliced**
1 teaspoon chili paste or 1–2 red chilies, finely
** minced**
scant 3 tablespoons top-quality fish sauce

Open the oysters. Keep each one in the half shell.

Blanch the spinach in lightly salted boiling water just until it wilts. Drain, refresh in iced water, drain and squeeze dry, then shred very finely. Blanch the mushrooms, shred very finely and set aside.

To prepare the **lime and lemon grass dressing**, stir the sugar with the lime or lemon juice until dissolved. Wash the cilantro thoroughly and pat dry. Cut off the roots and 2 inches of the stems, reserving the leaves for some other use. Mince the cilantro roots and stems very finely and add together with all the other dressing ingredients to the lemon juice. Mix well and set aside for at least 15 minutes. If preferred, the dressing can be made several hours in advance.

Just before the oysters are required, put a little of the spinach and sliced mushrooms on top of each oyster in its half shell. Broil the oysters for 2–3 minutes under a moderately hot broiler, until just cooked. Top with the prepared dressing and sliced red chili, if desired. Serve immediately.

Helpful hint: The reserved cilantro leaves will keep for up to 1 week if wrapped in a paper towel and refrigerated in an airtight container.

YAM AND MACADAMIA CROQUETTES

Beh Kim Un, Shakahari, Melbourne

Surprisingly simple to make, this crunchy, flavorful combination of steamed Asian tubers, macadamia nuts and seasonings can be served as an appetizer or featured as a main course for vegetarians. Canned salted (pickled) mustard greens (known in Cantonese as *ham choy*) are available in any Chinese food store.

$1/3$ cup vegetable oil
1 medium-sized onion, finely sliced
3 cloves garlic, very finely chopped
7 ounces roasted unsalted macadamia nuts
    ($1^1/_2$ cups), coarsely crushed
4 teaspoons dried red pepper flakes
$1/2$ cup finely sliced long beans
$1/2$ cup finely sliced salted mustard greens
10 ounces yam, steamed until soft, peeled and
    mashed ($1^1/_2$ cups)
5 ounces cassava (tapioca root) or potato,
    steamed until soft, peeled and mashed ($3/_4$ cup)
4 teaspoons chopped palm sugar (preferably
    coconut)
scant 3 tablespoons rice flour
salt to taste
oil for pan frying

Cilantro Coconut Sauce:

6 fresh cilantro plants
1–2 red chilies, finely sliced
$1/2$ cup lemon juice
2 cups water
2 cloves garlic, sliced

$3^1/_2$ ounces palm sugar (preferably
    coconut), chopped (about $1/2$ cup)
$1/2$ cup toasted dried coconut
salt to taste

Heat the oil and gently stir fry the onion until transparent. Add the garlic and cook for a few seconds, then put in the macadamia nuts and red pepper flakes. Stir fry for 2 minutes, then add the long beans and salted mustard greens. Stir fry for another 2 minutes, then add all remaining ingredients, except oil, stirring to mix well. Transfer to a bowl and allow to cool.

Prepare the **cilantro coconut sauce**. Finely chop the roots and 2 inches of the cilantro stems. Measure $1/2$ cup of cilantro leaves and reserve the remainder for some other dish. Put the cilantro roots and stems into a heavy-bottomed pan, add the chilies, lemon juice, water, garlic and palm sugar. Cook, stirring from time to time, until the mixture has reduced by half. Transfer to a blender, add the cilantro leaves and dried coconut and process to make a purée. Set aside.

Just before the dish is required, shape the yam and macadamia mixture into small croquettes. Heat a little oil in a frying pan until very hot, then fry the croquettes on both sides until golden brown. Serve hot with the cilantro coconut sauce.

SCALLOPS WITH BLACK-BEAN VINAIGRETTE

Tetsuya Wakuda, Tetsuya's, Sydney

A mixture of typically Asian seasonings with extra-virgin olive oil makes an unusual vinaigrette for this excellent appetizer. Although the recipe calls for large fresh scallops, raw shrimp could be substituted.

16 fresh raw scallops, or 16 large shrimp, peeled and halved
a sprinkle of olive oil
salt and freshly ground black pepper to taste
finely shredded toasted laver (*nori*)
1 average-sized leek (white part only), cut in julienne shreds and deep-fried in olive oil
***ogo* seaweed (optional)**

Vinaigrette:
¼ cup salted black beans
¼ cup very finely chopped shallots
2 tablespoons very finely chopped ginger root
1 clove garlic, very finely chopped
¼ cup extra-virgin olive oil
3 tablespoons rice wine vinegar
scant 2 tablespoons *mirin*
1 teaspoon light soy sauce

Whisk all **vinaigrette** ingredients together and set aside. Clean and dry the scallops. Smear a non-stick frying pan with olive oil and heat. Sear the scallops or shrimp on both sides, taking great care not to over-cook them.

Put about 1 heaped tablespoonful of *nori* onto each plate and top with 4 scallops or 8 shrimp halves. Spoon over a little of the vinaigrette and top with a garnish of deep-fried leeks. Spread a little *ogo* seaweed around the base of the scallops if using.

FOUR DANCES OF THE SEA

Cheong Liew, The Grange Restaurant, Adelaide Hilton

This poetically named appetizer consists of 4 different dishes, each served in tiny portions on a plate. The result is as exquisite from a taste point of view as it is visually. Although all 4 dishes harmonize when served together, there is no reason why you should not serve just 1 or 2 as an appetizer. The recipes will serve 6 portions. Serve at room temperature, not chilled.

SOUSED SNOOK

10 ounces freshest possible snook fillet, or other fine white-fleshed fish
4 teaspoons sea salt
4 teaspoons sugar
$^1/_2$ cup rice vinegar
3 tablespoons *sake*
3 tablespoons *mirin*
6 slices avocado

Opposite:
*Glass platter by
Natasha Fogel,
Balmain Market,
Sydney.*

Wasabi Mayonnaise:

1 egg yolk
1 teaspoon Japanese horseradish powder (*wasabi*)
4 teaspoons rice vinegar
$^1/_2$ cup warm peanut oil
3 tablespoons sugar syrup (made by boiling together equal quantities of sugar and water)

Prepare the ***wasabi* mayonnaise** by whisking the egg yolk, *wasabi* powder and vinegar together. Pour in the peanut oil gradually, whisking until the mixture thickens. Add the sugar syrup, mix well and set aside.

Clean and trim the fish, removing any bones. Try to remove the clear outer membrane but leave on the skin. Sprinkle the fish on both sides with salt and sugar and lay, skin side down, in a dish. Marinate in the refrigerator for 2 hours. Combine the vinegar, *sake*, and *mirin* and sprinkle over the fish. Leave to marinate for at least 1 more hour.

To serve, slice the fillets at an angle diagonally and serve 3 slices per person. Cut each slice of avocado in two and fan out on the plates, adding a tablespoonful of mayonnaise. Garnish if desired with a little shredded *wakame* seaweed.

CUTTLEFISH SASHIMI WITH SQUID-INK NOODLES

6 ounces freshest possible cuttlefish
10 ounces fine flat squid ink noodles or Japanese buckwheat noodles (*soba* or *cha-soba*), cooked, drained and chilled
scant 3 tablespoons sunflower seed oil
4 teaspoons balsamic vinegar
4 teaspoons light soy sauce
4 teaspoons *mirin*

SALAD OF TURNIPS AND ROASTED TOMATOES

Paul Merrony, Merrony's, Sydney

An unusual yet simple appetizer, this combines turnips with tomatoes and a vinaigrette dressing. Sometimes regarded as a rather old-fashioned vegetable, turnips have a distinctive flavor that is enhanced in this recipe.

15 medium-sized ripe tomatoes, blanched and peeled
salt and pepper to taste
1 small bunch fresh thyme
2 teaspoons olive oil
2 large turnips
1½ tablespoons finely sliced chives

Vinaigrette:

1 teaspoon coriander seeds
1 heaped tablespoon honey
3½ tablespoons white wine vinegar
2 teaspoons French mustard
3½ tablespoons olive oil
3½ tablespoons mild vegetable oil
salt and pepper to taste

Opposite:
Cutlery from Ventura Design, Sydney; plates by Sally Hunter and napkin ring by Jane Ruljancich from The Crafts Council, The Rocks, Sydney.

Cut the tomatoes into quarters, then remove the seeds with small sharp knife. Place a sheet of waxed paper on a flat oven tray and sprinkle with a little salt and pepper. Lay the deseeded tomatoes flat side down on the paper and season with salt and pepper. Sprinkle with the thyme, then drizzle the olive oil over the tomatoes. Bake at 325°F for 20–30 minutes. This step can be done the day before the dish is required, but as the salad is served at room temperature, the tomatoes must be removed from the refrigerator well in advance.

Peel the turnips and then cut with a mandoline into thin slices. You should have about 80 disks of 1½ inches in diameter. Lightly blanch the turnip slices in boiling salted water and when just cooked, drain, refresh in iced water and drain again. Refrigerate until required.

To make the **vinaigrette**, put the coriander seeds and honey into a small saucepan and cook until light golden brown. Add the vinegar, then transfer the contents of the saucepan to a bowl. Allow to cool, then whisk in the mustard. When fully emulsified, slowly add the oils in a thin stream, whisking constantly. Season with salt and pepper and set aside.

To assemble the dish, fold each piece of tomato in half and place on top of a turnip slice. Cover the tomato with another turnip slice. Repeat until you have a stack of 4 turnip slices and 3 tomato pieces. This will make 20 "mini-salads."

Put 5 turnip/tomato salads on each of 4 serving plates. Dress the salad with the vinaigrette and sprinkle with chives. Serve at room temperature.

TEA-SMOKED TUNA WITH SWEET-SOUR FENNEL SALAD

Christine Manfield, The Paramount Restaurant, Sydney

The Chinese tea-smoking method is used for tuna in this appetizer, which serves 6.

6 pieces of $^3/_4$ -inch-thick belly tuna, weighing about 4 ounces each
4 tablespoons tea–smoking mixture (page 134)
1 long thin cucumber, about 1–1$^1/_4$ inches in diameter
1 cup (tightly packed) very finely sliced fennel bulb
2 small Asian eggplants, roasted, peeled and sliced
sweet and sour dressing (page 135)
scant 3 tablespoons very finely diced red onion
scant 3 tablespoons pickled ginger slices, sliced in fine shreds
2 teaspoons basil leaves, finely sliced
12 small radicchio leaves
18 Belgian endive leaves

Line a large wok with foil and place over high heat. While the wok is heating, lay a sheet of waxed paper across a steaming basket that fits neatly over the wok. Pierce the paper in several places around the outside with a skewer to allow the smoke to circulate. Lay the tuna pieces on the paper, making sure they do not touch. It may be necessary to do 2 batches to ensure even smoking.

Spread the prepared tea-smoking mixture over the foil in the base of the wok. When this starts to heat and burn at the edges, place the tuna-filled steaming basket over the top and cover with a tight-fitting lid. (Do this under an exhaust vent to avoid filling your kitchen with smoke.) Smoke the tuna for 4 minutes, remove the lid and turn the tuna over. Replace the lid and smoke for another 2 minutes. It must not be smoked for too long as this produces a high tannin content and bitter taste. Remove the steamer from the wok immediately. Wrap up the burnt remains of the tea-smoking mixture in the foil and discard.

Take the tuna out of the steamer and leave until it is cool enough to handle. Slice the tuna along the grain, then cut into dice. It should be cooked on the outside and very pink and rare in the center.

Peel the cucumber and shave into long strips with a vegetable peeler, discarding the core of seeds. Put the cucumber and fennel slices in half of the sweet and sour dressing for 3 minutes.

Combine the smoked tuna and eggplant in the remaining sweet and sour dressing and marinate for 1 minute. Combine the marinated cucumber and fennel with the tuna and eggplant and add all other ingredients, mixing carefully to ensure even distribution. Pile on 6 serving plates and serve immediately. (This salad should not be chilled.)

TURKEY SALAD WITH TAMARILLO AND MANGO

Kurt Looser, San Francisco Grill, Sydney Hilton

The intense flavor and acidity of the tamarillo, a deep red, egg-shaped fruit, which used to be known in some countries as the tree tomato, provides a contrast to the sweetness of fresh mango in this quickly prepared turkey salad.

4 tamarillos, blanched in boiling water, peeled and sliced
2 ripe mangoes, peeled and sliced
8–10 leaves butter lettuce
8 leaves green oak leaf lettuce
4 leaves red leaf lettuce
8 ounces smoked turkey roll, thinly sliced
1 heaped tablespoon toasted slivered almonds

Dressing:
$^1/_2$ cup almond, hazelnut or walnut oil
$2^1/_2$ tablespoons white wine vinegar
$5^1/_2$ tablespoons crushed almonds
salt and pepper to taste

Combine all the **dressing** ingredients, mixing well.

Arrange the sliced mangoes and tamarillos in the center of a large platter or on 4 individual salad plates. Toss the butter and green oak lettuce with a little of the dressing and arrange on top of the fruit. Arrange slices of smoked turkey on top and garnish with the red leaf lettuce. Sprinkle with more dressing and scatter the almonds on top.

Opposite:
Salad servers from Orson & Blake Collectables, Woollahra, Sydney; salad bowl from David Hislop, Paddington Bazaar, Sydney; glassware and pewter bowl from Mexico, Paddington, Sydney.

SPICED CHICKEN WITH LENTIL SALAD

Damien Pignolet, Bistro Moncur, Sydney

6 small to medium-sized skinless chicken
   breasts
1 clove garlic, bruised
scant 3 tablespoons *Quatre Épices* (page 134)
$1^1/_4$ cups or more olive oil (see below)
5 sprigs fresh thyme
dressing for lentil salad (page 135)
2 stalks celery, cut in julienne shreds $1^1/_4$
   inches long
1 bunch arugula, torn into small pieces
finely grated rind of 2 lemons
3 shallots, peeled and finely chopped
3 heaped tablespoons finely chopped parsley

Lentil Salad:

$1^1/_2$ cups brown lentils
1 small onion, quartered lengthwise
1 small carrot, sliced
1 bay leaf
$^1/_2$ teaspoon salt
chicken stock or water

For best results, start preparing the chicken only 3 hours prior to serving to avoid refrigeration and ensure maximum flavor and texture. Dry the chicken breasts with a paper towel. Rub the inside of a bowl with the garlic and put in the *quatre épices*. Rub the chicken in this, turning the pieces over to ensure they are covered on all sides. Set aside at room temperature.

To prepare the **lentil salad**, cover the lentils with boiling water and leave until the water has cooled. Drain off the water, add a second batch of boiling water and repeat. After a total of 30 minutes' soaking, drain and put in a pan with the onion, carrot, bay leaf and salt. Cover with chicken stock or water and simmer until tender but not soft and mushy. Drain and discard the carrot, onion and bay leaf. Set aside.

Heat oil in a pan into which the chicken breast will fit. Put in the garlic clove used to rub the bowl and the thyme. Add the chicken and cook at a low temperature for 20 minutes. It is essential that the chicken should poach gently in the oil rather than deep-fry. Test the chicken after 20 minutes with a skewer to see if the juices run clear. If not, return and cook for another 5–10 minutes. Remove the pan from the heat and allow the chicken to cool slightly in the oil, then drain thoroughly. Cut the chicken in fine slices across the breast.

To serve the dish, choose a wide deep platter or bowl. Put two-thirds of the dressing in the bottom, add the lentils and celery, then put in the arugula and add the sliced chicken. Pour over the remaining dressing. Combine the grated lemon rind, shallots and parsley and scatter over the salad. Grind some black pepper over the top and place on the table. Toss well immediately before serving.

LETTUCE AND FRIED SQUID WITH BLACK-BEAN DRESSING

Herbert Franceschini, Victoria's Restaurant, Brisbane Hilton

A mixture of small lettuce leaves makes a bed for deep-fried squid dressed with an East-West dressing where Chinese black beans, soy sauce and sesame oil are partnered with European olive oil and balsamic vinegar.

10 ounces small lettuce leaves such as arugula, chicory, romaine, frisée, oak leaf lettuce, butter lettuce
1 small to medium-sized red bell pepper
1½ pounds small fresh squid
2 cups white flour
1 teaspoon salt
1 teaspoon freshly ground black pepper
4 teaspoons paprika
olive oil for deep-frying

Black-bean Dressing:

1 clove garlic, lightly bruised
5 tablespoons plus 1 teaspoon balsamic vinegar
¼ teaspoon salt
a little freshly ground black pepper
1 teaspoon black-bean and chili sauce (available from Chinese food stores)
1 teaspoon fermented black beans, rinsed and finely chopped
pinch of sugar
scant 3 tablespoons sesame oil
scant 3 tablespoons olive oil
5 tablespoons plus 1 teaspoon light soy sauce

Opposite:
Glass platter by Natasha Fogel, Balmain Market, Sydney.

Prepare the **black-bean dressing** in advance by putting the garlic in a jar with the vinegar, salt and pepper. Set aside for several hours to allow the flavors to blend. Discard the garlic and add black-bean and chili sauce, chopped black beans and sugar. Slowly whisk in both types of oil. Store at room temperature until required.

Wash the lettuce leaves and dry thoroughly. Wrap in a clean towel and refrigerate until required.

Cut the pepper into fine julienne shreds and put in a bowl of iced water. Leave in the fridge for about 1 hour until they curl.

Peel the skin off the squid, clean thoroughly and dry with paper towels. Cut the squid into rings; if desired, trim off the long straggling ends of the squid tentacles, and discard the top beaky portion. Combine the flour, salt, pepper and paprika in a plastic bag. Add some of the squid rings (and the tentacles if using) and shake in the bag to coat with the flour. Lift the squid out and shake in a sieve or colander to dislodge excess flour. Repeat with the remaining squid.

Heat the oil until very hot and deep-fry the squid, a little at a time, until golden brown. Drain.

Toss the lettuce leaves with the prepared dressing and serve with the squid placed on top. Garnish with the pepper curls.

SQUASH AND YABBY BROTH WITH SEAFOOD RAVIOLI

Werner Kimmeringer, Cliveden Room, Melbourne Hilton

4 golden nugget winter squash, each about the size of a large grapefruit

12 yabbies or medium-sized raw shrimp, blanched in boiling salted water

3 tablespoons olive oil

1 average-sized leek, bottom white and pale green portion only, chopped

1 stalk celery, chopped

1 red onion, chopped

2 cloves garlic, chopped

1 pound winter squash (preferably butternut), peeled and soft stringy pulp discarded, flesh cut into $1\frac{1}{4}$ -inch cubes or balls

1 cup dry white wine

4 cups clear fish stock

2 bay leaves

$\frac{1}{2}$ teaspoon white peppercorns

1 whole star anise

pinch of saffron strands

salt and pepper to taste

ravioli dough (page 135)

ravioli filling (page 135)

Slice the tops off the golden nugget squash and remove the seeds, pulp and any soft parts. Carve the rims decoratively with a small knife. Steam or blanch in boiling salted water until just cooked. Do not over-cook as the squash must be firm enough to be used as a container. Drain and set aside.

Peel the yabbies or shrimp. Keep 4 aside for garnishing the finished dish and use the remainder for the ravioli filling.

Heat the oil in a saucepan and add the yabby shells and heads, leek, celery, onion, garlic and cubed squash. Sauté gently until the yabby shells take color and the onion softens, taking care not to let the onion turn brown. Add the white wine and stir to deglaze the pan, then put in the fish stock, herbs, saffron and season with salt and pepper to taste. Bring to a boil, lower heat and simmer uncovered, removing any scum that might rise to the top. After the stock has cooked 20 minutes, leave to rest for 30 minutes and then remove carefully with a ladle, pouring through a fine sieve into a clean pan. Set aside.

Roll out the prepared ravioli dough until very thin and cut into 2 rectangles, each measuring about 8 inches x 6 inches. Divide the ravioli filling into 8 portions. On one sheet of ravioli dough, place the portions of filling at even intervals. Cover with the second sheet of dough and push down between the mounds of ravioli filling to make the two sheets of dough adhere. Cut around each mound with a 2-inch cookie cutter.

Blanch the ravioli in boiling salted water. Place 1 steamed squash into each serving bowl. Reheat the reserved stock and pour into the squash. Put 2 ravioli into each squash, and garnish each with 1 of the reserved yabbies.

DUCK EGG PASTA, TROUT AND TOMATO BUTTER SAUCE

Alla Wolf-Tasker, The Lakehouse, Daylesford, Victoria

The fresh produce of the countryside surrounding the Lakehouse inspired this excellent combination, which serves 6 as an appetizer or 4 as a main course.

6 stems of fresh dill
8 ounces ripe tomatoes
1¼ cups fish stock
3 tablespoons dry white wine
splash of light cream
¼ cup tiny capers
1 smoked trout, weighing 10-12 ounces, skinned, boned and broken into chunks
14 tablespoons unsalted butter, diced

Pasta:

2¾ cups white flour
1 duck egg, lightly beaten
pinch of salt
4 teaspoons olive oil
1½ cups fish stock
⅔ cup light cream

Opposite:
*Trout supplied by
Aqua Farms
Australia Pty Ltd,
Bulleen, Victoria.
Cutlery by
Villeroy and
Boch, French's
Forest, Sydney.*

Prepare the **pasta** by combining the flour, egg, salt and oil until smooth. Form into a ball and roll out into a sheet either by hand or with a pasta machine. Cut the dough into strips about 1¼ inches wide and at least 10 inches long. Cook the pasta in a large pot of salted boiling water for 3–5 minutes, until just cooked, then drain and plunge into iced water to stop the cooking process. Drain and toss with a little olive oil, then set aside. Bring the stock and cream to a boil, then simmer uncovered until reduced by half. Keep this aside to reheat the pasta just before serving.

Reserve 6 sprigs of dill as a garnish and finely chop the remainder. Peel the tomatoes, halve and remove the seeds. Cut the flesh into fine dice and set aside, putting the tomato skins, seeds and any juice that has run out during the preparation into a saucepan. Add the fish stock and white wine, then boil rapidly, uncovered, until it has reduced to one-third. Strain the liquid and add a splash of cream. Return to a cleaned pan and simmer until thick. Set aside.

Add the dill, diced tomato, capers, smoked trout and pasta to the sauce made for reheating the pasta. Toss and heat until the liquid has reduced and the ingredients have heated through.

Reheat the tomato sauce over low heat, then gradually add the diced butter, stirring to bind the sauce. When all of the butter is incorporated, remove from the heat and whisk a little to ensure the sauce is properly emulsified. Adjust seasoning to taste.

Divide the pasta among 6 bowls and pour over some of the sauce. Garnish with dill and serve hot.

CRAB TORTELLI

Bill Marchetti, Marchetti's Latin, Melbourne

6 pounds live mud crabs
12 cups water
$1\frac{1}{4}$ cups dry white wine
1 pound of mixed celery, carrot, and onion,
    chopped (about $1\frac{1}{4}$ cups each)
4 bay leaves
handful of parsley stalks
1 teaspoon black peppercorns
scant 3 tablespoons salt
handful of fennel tops (optional)
3 tablespoons butter
$\frac{1}{2}$ cup very finely diced onion
Béchamel Sauce (page 135)
4 teaspoons chopped parsley
scant 3 tablespoons grated Parmesan
pinch of cayenne pepper
salt and pepper to taste
pasta dough (page 135)
2 egg yolks, stirred
butter sauce (page 136)
scant 3 tablespoons finely chopped chives
freshly ground black pepper

Place the crabs in the freezer for a couple of hours to kill them. Put the water, wine, chopped vegetables, bay leaves, parsley, pepper, salt and fennel tops into a very large saucepan and bring to a boil. Cover, lower the temperature and simmer for 30 minutes. Add the crabs, bring the liquid back to a boil and simmer the crabs for 20 minutes. Remove the crabs from the pan and allow to cool for an hour before extracting the meat and discarding all traces of cartilage. Chop $\frac{3}{4}$ pound of the crabmeat (3 cups) and save the remainder for garnish.

Heat the butter in a heavy pan and sauté the diced onion until transparent. Add the chopped crabmeat and sauté for 2 minutes. Add the béchamel sauce, parsley, Parmesan cheese, cayenne pepper, salt and pepper, mixing well. Turn the mixture onto a greased plastic tray and cover with buttered waxed paper.

Cut circles of pasta dough with a $2\frac{1}{2}$-inch cutter. Brush the edge of one circle with the stirred egg yolks and place a soup spoon full of the crab mixture in the center. Place another circle of dough on top and press around the edges. Repeat until all the circles of dough are used up. Place the tortelli in a single layer on a flat tray covered with waxed paper.

Bring a large pan of salted water to a boil and add the tortelli. Cook for about 5 minutes. Check one tortelli, making sure the edges where it has been sealed are thoroughly cooked. Remove the tortelli carefully with a slotted spoon, drain and toss in the butter sauce. Sprinkle with chopped chives, black pepper and reserved crabmeat and serve immediately.

RAVIOLI OF LOBSTER WITH TOMATO AND BASIL

Tetsuya Wakuda, Tetsuya's, Sydney

These delicate ravioli are stuffed with lobster and scallops, although a combination of shrimp and good-quality white fish could be used, if preferred. It is important to chill the seafood and cream thoroughly before making the ravioli filling.

$^1/_2$ **pound raw scallops or peeled raw shrimp, chilled**
$^1/_3$ **teaspoon finely chopped fresh tarragon**
4 teaspoons finely chopped chives
1 egg white
1$^1/_4$ cups cream, chilled
salt and black pepper to taste
$^1/_2$ **pound cooked lobster meat or white fish fillet, finely diced and chilled**
Japanese seaweed (*wakame* and *ogo*) to garnish
24 *gow gee* or *won ton* wrappers
24 $^3/_4$ -inch squares toasted laver (*nori*)
1 tablespoon vegetable oil
4 teaspoons flying fish roe or red lumpfish roe to garnish

Tomato and Basil Dressing:

7 tablespoons extra-virgin olive oil
2 tablespoons rice vinegar
$^1/_2$ **cup finely diced peeled tomato**
1 teaspoon coriander powder
$^1/_2$ **teaspoon finely chopped basil**
$^1/_4$ **teaspoon finely chopped garlic**
salt and white pepper to taste
pinch of sugar

Chop the scallops or shrimp coarsely and blend to a paste with the tarragon, chives and egg white, gradually adding the cream in a thin stream while the motor is still running. When the cream is incorporated, season with salt and pepper. Stir in the lobster or fish and leave to chill.

Prepare the **tomato and basil dressing** by stirring all ingredients together. Prepare the *wakame* and *ogo* seaweeds by rinsing and soaking separately in cold water for 10 minutes. Drain thoroughly and shred the *wakame* finely.

Lay out the *gow gee* or *won ton* wrappers and top each with a square of *nori*. Put a spoonful of the seafood filling in the center of each. Wet the edges of the wrapper with a finger dipped in water and lay another piece of *gow gee* on top, pressing the edges gently to seal.

Bring a large saucepan of salted water to a boil, then add the vegetable oil and ravioli. Lower the heat to just below boiling and gently simmer the ravioli for about 5 minutes; it is important not to let the water boil rapidly or it will spoil the texture and appearance of the ravioli. Drain the cooked ravioli.

Put some shredded *wakame* on the bottom of each plate, top with ravioli and pour over the prepared sauce. Garnish with a little *ogo* seaweed and 1 teaspoon of flying fish roe per serving.

CRAB SALAD ON BUCKWHEAT NOODLES

Stephanie Alexander, Stephanie's, Melbourne

Inspired by the refreshing chilled buckwheat noodles popular in Japan during summertime, this combination of seasoned crabmeat with dressed noodles makes an excellent starter to a meal.

1/2 **pound fresh crabmeat**
1/2 **pound buckwheat noodles (*soba*)**
4 **teaspoons lemon juice**
4 **teaspoons extra-virgin olive oil**
4 **teaspoons freshly chopped parsley**
1 **teaspoon black sesame seeds**
scant 3 **tablespoons chopped cilantro leaves and fine stems**

Dressing:

4 **tablespoons light soy sauce**
scant 1/2 **cup Chinese red rice vinegar**
2 **tablespoons sesame oil**
2 **tablespoons *mirin***
2 **teaspoons very finely chopped ginger root**
2 **teaspoons very finely chopped garlic**
1 **teaspoon very finely chopped red chili**

Vegetable Garnish:

1 **leek, cut in 3-inch-long julienne shreds**
1 **carrot, cut in 3-inch-long julienne shreds**
2 **pieces of ginger root, each 2**1/2 **inches long, cut in julienne shreds**
oil for deep-frying

Pick over the crabmeat carefully, discarding any cartilage and shell. Reserve the crabmeat.

Bring a large saucepan of unsalted water to a boil and add the noodles. Stir to prevent them from sticking and after 4 minutes, add 1 cup of cold water and stir again until the water reboils. When the noodles are properly cooked (not firm or *al dente*), drain in a colander, rinse under cold running water and drain again.

Combine all **dressing** ingredients, mixing well, and moisten the cooked noodles with a little of this. Refrigerate the noodles until required.

Prepare the **vegetable garnish** by deep-frying each vegetable separately in hot oil until crisp. Drain on paper towels. When all vegetables are cooked, mix together lightly and keep dry and warm.

To serve, season the crab with lemon juice, oil and parsley. Season the noodles with the sesame seeds, chopped cilantro and plenty of the dressing. Coil a nest of noodles on each of 4 plates and place a mound of dressed crab on top.

Garnish with a topknot of vegetable garnish. If desired, deep-fried parsnip chips can be used as an additional garnish. (Stephanie's own Watermelon Rind Pickle is used as an additional garnish in the photograph.)

EGGPLANT, RICOTTA AND SAFFRON CUSTARD TART

Marieke Brugman, Howqua Dale Gourmet Retreat, Mansfield, Victoria

2 cups white flour
14 tablespoons unsalted butter, cut in pea-sized
  dice
$\frac{1}{2}$ cup sour cream (35% fat content)
saffron custard (page 136)

Filling:
  1$\frac{1}{2}$–2 pounds eggplant
  scant 3 tablespoons salt
  $\frac{1}{4}$ cup olive oil
  6 large red onions, thinly sliced
  8 ounces goat cheese or regular ricotta, or firm
    chèvre cheese

Make the pastry by combining the flour, butter and sour cream in a food processor and pulsing just until the mixture forms a ball around the blade. Remove, pat into a disk and cover with plastic film. Refrigerate for 1 hour, then roll out on a very lightly floured board. Choose a 12-inch or 13-inch metal tart pan with a removable base. Fit the rolled-out pastry into the pan and cover the top of the pastry with a circle of non-stick baking paper (preferably coated). Cover with a circle of aluminum foil and fill with dry beans. Return the pastry to the refrigerator until needed; it can be kept for up to 24 hours.

Prepare the **filling** by slicing the eggplant lengthwise into 5 or 6 slices. Sprinkle with salt and set aside in a colander for 1 hour. Wash the eggplant slices and dry thoroughly, then paint both sides with a little of the olive oil. Broil under moderate heat until tender and golden brown on both sides. Remove and drain on paper towels.

Heat the remaining oil and cook the onions over very low heat, stirring from time to time, until they are brown and caramelized. Drain in a sieve and reserve the oil for a vinaigrette.

Heat the oven to 425°F and bake the prepared tart base for 10 minutes. Remove the beans, foil and baking paper and cook for another 10 minutes until golden. Remove from the oven and immediately fan out a layer of eggplant over the pastry. Intersperse with caramelized onion and dabs of the ricotta. Repeat with a second layer. Carefully pour in the saffron custard, set the tart pan on a baking sheet and return to the oven, heat now reduced to 300°F.

Bake the tart for 45–60 minutes, until set. The custard must not swell. Rest the cooked tart for at least 10 minutes before slicing.

Serve with a salad of greens dressed tossed with a vinaigrette made from the olive oil used to caramelize the onions, beaten with a dash of balsamic or red wine vinegar.

EGGPLANT WITH POLENTA AND BUSH TOMATO SALSA

Paul Hoeps, Breezes Restaurant, Cairns Hilton

An ideal dish for a vegetarian meal, alternating slices of polenta and eggplant are given extra flavor by a sauce made with native bush tomatoes.

1 large eggplant (about 1 pound), cut cross-
    wise in $^1/_2$ -inch slices, skin left on
salt
1 cup milk
$^1/_2$–1 cup olive oil
bush tomato salsa (page 136)
4 tablespoons chopped basil
1 red bell pepper, finely diced
$^1/_2$ cup sweet corn kernels
1 teaspoon chopped oregano
4 ounces mozzarella cheese, sliced
12 whole basil leaves, deep-fried until crisp

Polenta:

$^3/_4$ cup fine polenta
2 cups milk
1 clove garlic, very finely chopped
2 teaspoons grated Parmesan cheese
4 egg yolks

Prepare the **polenta** first by combining the polenta, milk and garlic in a saucepan (preferably non-stick). Bring to a boil and simmer, stirring constantly, for 10 minutes. Stir in the cheese, remove from the heat and allow to cool slightly. Beat in the egg yolks and spread on a waxed-paper-lined 8-inch x 12-inch baking dish. Leave to set.

Opposite:
Plates from Rose Wallis Studio, Sydney.

Salt the sliced eggplant liberally and leave in a colander for 30 minutes. Rinse under running water and soak in milk for 10 minutes. Heat $^1/_4$ cup of the olive oil and fry the eggplant slices on both sides until golden brown. Add a little more oil if necessary.

Cut the polenta into circles the same size as the eggplant slices. Put a polenta slice on a baking dish greased with a little olive oil. Top with a tablespoonful of the bush tomato salsa and a slice of fried eggplant. Sprinkle with a little chopped basil and add another slice of polenta, some more salsa and another slice of fried eggplant. Top with a slice of mozzarella. Repeat until all the polenta and eggplant is used up. Bake in a 350° oven for 10 minutes.

While the polenta and eggplant are baking, heat 1 tablespoon of the remaining olive oil and sauté the pepper, corn and oregano until the pepper is tender.

To serve, put a tower of polenta and eggplant in the center of each plate and garnish with the sautéed pepper and corn. Top with deep-fried basil leaves.

SPINACH AND MUSHROOM RISOTTO

Bethany Finn, The Grange Brasserie, Adelaide Hilton

A mixture of Italian Arborio rice (the only type which makes a really good risotto) with mushrooms and spinach makes an ideal vegetarian main course (if the pancetta is omitted) or can accompany a veal or poultry dish if preferred.

4 very thin slices pancetta or prosciutto (optional)
7 tablespoons olive oil
2 large onions, cut in $\frac{1}{2}$-inch dice
5 cloves garlic, finely chopped
2 cups Arborio rice
4 pounds Swiss brown mushrooms or field mushrooms
$\frac{1}{2}$ cup grated Parmesan cheese
chopped fresh basil to taste
sea salt and freshly ground black pepper to taste
12 ounces spinach, blanched
8 small abalone mushrooms, sautéed in a little olive oil until cooked

Mushroom Stock:

4 tablespoons olive oil
2 onions, roughly chopped
5 cloves garlic, sliced
2 sprigs fresh thyme
4 pounds mixed mushrooms, washed, drained and chopped
4 cups vegetable stock

Prepare the **mushroom stock** first. Heat the oil in a saucepan and sauté the onions, garlic and thyme until the onions are transparent. Add the mushrooms and sauté until the juice starts to come out. Put in the vegetable stock, bring to a boil, cover and simmer for 10 minutes. Strain and reserve the stock, keeping it warm.

Lay the pancetta or prosciutto slices on a baking sheet and bake in a 400°F oven for about 5 minutes, until the pancetta is crispy. Keep aside as a garnish.

Heat the olive oil and sauté the onions and garlic until transparent, then add the rice and sauté until it is thoroughly coated with the oil. Add the Swiss brown or field mushrooms and mushroom stock, stirring in gently. Cover the pan with waxed or greaseproof paper and stand over medium heat for about 14 minutes so that the rice absorbs all the liquid and is cooked through. The grains should be chewy but not crunchy. Add the Parmesan cheese, basil, salt and pepper to taste, lastly folding in the spinach.

Garnish with 2 abalone mushrooms and 1 slice of crisp pancetta per person, if using.

SNAPPER AND SHRIMP MOUSSE IN NORI OMELET

Christine Manfield, The Paramount Restaurant, Sydney

1¼ pounds snapper fillet, skinned and boned
shrimp mousse (page 136)
2 bunches spinach, washed, stems
　　removed and leaves blanched
2 tablespoons unsalted butter
sea salt to taste
freshly ground black pepper to taste
shrimp sauce (page 136)
6 teaspoons fresh salmon roe

Nori Omelets:

3 large eggs
½ teaspoon sesame oil
½ teaspoon fish sauce
pinch of freshly ground black pepper
pinch sea salt
1 large sheet of toasted laver (*nori*), cut in strips

Prepare the **nori omelets** first. Whisk the eggs lightly, then add the sesame oil, fish sauce, pepper and salt. Gently stir in the *nori* strips with a fork. Heat a 6-inch non-stick pan over medium heat and brush the base of the pan with oil. Add just enough of the omelet mixture to coat the base of the pan, and cook until it begins to set. Remove the omelet and place on a flat surface. Repeat until the mixture is used up and you have 6 omelets, stacking them on top of each other as they cook. Cover with a kitchen cloth until ready to use.

Slice the snapper fillets into thin even slices and lay carefully over the 6 omelets. Spread the shrimp mousse across the snapper in a thick horizontal line and roll up each omelet. Cover with plastic film, rolling up like a sausage and keeping airtight, twisting the ends to keep firm. Rest in the refrigerator on a flat tray for 2 hours before cooking.

To cook the omelet-wrapped mousse, place in a steaming basket in a single layer, cover with a lid and steam over gently simmering water for 30 minutes, until the mousse is cooked and firm to the touch. Be sure to keep the water simmering only very gently as higher heat creates more steam which will cause the mousse to overcook and explode out of the omelet covering. When the mousse is cooked, remove from the steamer and rest on a board for 2 minutes. Remove the plastic film carefully and slice each omelet in half across the middle.

Heat the blanched spinach in the butter in a pan until warm, then season with a little salt and pepper and spoon onto the center of the serving plates. Sit 2 omelet halves on the spinach with the cut side facing up, and ladle some of the hot shrimp sauce around the base. Put ½ teaspoonful of salmon roe in the center of each omelet half and serve immediately. This recipe serves 6 as an appetizer.

SALMON BURGER ON VEGETABLE SPAGHETTI

Werner Kimmeringer, Cliveden Room, Melbourne Hilton

Tasmania's delicious reared salmon features in this recipe, where seasoned patties of chopped salmon are accompanied by vegetables cut into spaghetti shapes. The tangy bush tomato chutney and lemon butter sauce add richness and flavor.

$1\frac{1}{2}$ **pounds fresh salmon**
$\frac{1}{3}$ **cup chopped shallots**
1 teaspoon freshly snipped dill weed
2 teaspoons lemon juice
2 tablespoons cottage cheese
2 egg yolks
salt and freshly ground black pepper to taste
8 ounces puff pastry
vegetable oil for frying
1 large carrot
1 parsnip or turnip
1 average-sized leek (white part only)
$\frac{1}{2}$ **bunch fresh chives, cut in 3-inch lengths**
1 teaspoon butter
4 teaspoons sour cream
4 teaspoons fresh salmon roe
lemon butter sauce (page 137)
$\frac{1}{3}$ **cup bush tomato chutney (page 137)**

Remove all skin and bones from the salmon and cut the flesh into very small dice. Combine with the shallots, dill, lemon juice, cottage cheese, egg yolks, salt and pepper to taste. Mix well, then shape into 4 patties and set aside on a lightly oiled tray.

Roll out the puff pastry until very thin and cut into 4 circles 4 inches in diameter. Heat $\frac{3}{4}$ inch of oil in a pan until very hot. Fry the pastry disks for about 2–3 minutes on each side until crisp and golden brown. Drain on paper towels and set aside.

Use a Japanese vegetable cutting tool, if possible, to produce long thin spaghetti shapes from the carrot and parsnip, or cut into fine julienne strips by hand. Cut the leek into the same size. Blanch the vegetables in boiling water, drain and refresh. Just before serving, toss the blanched vegetables and chives in 1 teaspoon of butter to warm through, then season with salt and pepper.

Fry the salmon burgers over moderately high heat in a lightly oiled non-stick pan, turning so that they are crisp and golden on the outside but medium rare inside.

To serve, put some of the reheated vegetable spaghetti into the center of each of 4 plates, top with a salmon burger and add a teaspoon of sour cream and salmon roe to each. Cover with a circle of puff pastry and spoon the lemon butter sauce around the side. Place dots of bush tomato chutney on the plate or, if preferred, mix the bush chutney into the lemon butter sauce before putting it on the plate.

GRILLED SCAMPI WITH BASIL CREAM SAUCE

Beh Kim Un, Isthmus of Kra, Melbourne

A Thai-inspired seafood dish which doesn't turn its nose up at Western butter and cream. Try to use Thai basil leaves (*horapa*) for maximum flavor.

4–6 large scampi or very large tiger shrimp, or use small lobsters or slipper lobsters
2 cloves garlic, very finely minced
1 teaspoon white pepper
4 teaspoons top-quality fish sauce
$1/3$ cup clarified butter or ghee

Basil Cream Sauce:
$1/3$ cup vegetable oil
5 shallots, finely sliced
8 ounces small raw shrimp (heads and shells intact), washed, drained and coarsely chopped
4 teaspoons hot red pepper flakes
4 cups chicken stock
$1/2$ cup Thai basil leaves (*horapa*), thinly sliced
$2^1/2$ tablespoons fish sauce
$1/3$ cup coconut cream or dairy cream

Carefully remove the shells from the scampi or tiger shrimp, leaving the heads and final tail section intact. Remove the black intestinal tract. If using lobsters, cut in half lengthwise. Combine the garlic, pepper, fish sauce and melted butter. Pour over the seafood and leave to marinate for 30 minutes.

While the seafood is marinating, prepare the **basil cream sauce**. Heat the oil in a saucepan and sauté the shallots until golden brown. Add the chopped shrimp and stir fry until they change color and start to smell fragrant. Add the red pepper flakes, stir fry for 1 minute and then put in the chicken stock. Simmer, uncovered, until the stock has reduced by half. Strain the stock and keep warm until serving the seafood. (The remaining sauce ingredients will be added at this time.)

Broil the seafood under a broiler turned to maximum heat until just cooked. Bring the sauce to a boil, add the sliced basil, fish sauce and coconut or dairy cream. Reduce the heat and stir just to heat the cream through, but do not allow to boil.

Place the grilled seafood on serving dishes and pour over the basil cream sauce.

BARRAMUNDI WITH BOK CHOY AND LAKSA SAUCE

Allan Koh, Chinois, Melbourne

Australia's excellent fine white-fleshed barramundi fish is steamed with baby Chinese *bok choy* cabbage and served with a spicy Malaysian *laksa* sauce, a reduction of the gravy that normally accompanies the popular noodle dish referred to as *laksa* in that country and in Singapore. Be sure to use only the finest quality fresh fish.

1 pound barramundi or other white fish fillets, cut in 12 pieces

6 baby Chinese *bok choy* cabbage, halved lengthwise

Laksa Sauce:

$^1/_2$ red onion, chopped

1 stalk lemon grass, use bottom 4 inches only, finely sliced

$^3/_4$ **inch piece of fresh galangal, chopped**

$^1/_2$ **dried red chili, sliced and soaked to soften**

$^1/_4$–$^1/_2$ **cup oil**

1 teaspoon curry powder for fish

$^1/_4$ **teaspoon turmeric powder**

$^1/_4$ **teaspoon coriander powder**

$^1/_4$ **teaspoon cumin powder**

$^1/_4$ **teaspoon paprika**

$^1/_4$ **teaspoon dried shrimp paste**

$^1/_2$ **cup coconut milk**

$^1/_4$ **cup fish stock**

$^1/_2$–1 **teaspoon sugar, to taste**

$^1/_4$–$^1/_2$ **teaspoon salt, to taste**

Prepare the **laksa sauce** first. Put the onion, lemon grass, galangal and chili in a blender and process until fine, adding a little of the oil if necessary to keep the blades turning. Heat the remaining oil in a saucepan and sauté the ground ingredients over moderate heat until fragrant; this should take 3–5 minutes. Add the curry powder, turmeric, coriander, cumin, paprika and shrimp paste and continue sautéing until the mixture smells fragrant. Slowly stir in the coconut milk, then add the fish stock and heat through. Season to taste with sugar and salt, and set aside.

On a heat-proof dish, alternate pieces of the fish and halves of the *bok choy*, overlapping slightly. Put inside a steamer and cook over boiling water for about 5–7 minutes, until cooked but not mushy and overcooked. (There is no need to season the fish as the *laksa* sauce will add flavor later.)

When the fish is cooked, gently reheat the *laksa* sauce but do not allow it to boil. Pour around the fish and *bok choy* and serve immediately.

CRISP-SKIN SALMON WITH A MOROCCAN TOUCH

Stephanie Alexander, Stephanie's, Melbourne

½ cup olive oil
4 medium-sized onions, sliced
2 large red bell peppers, each cut into 4 pieces
2 large yellow bell peppers, each cut into
    4 pieces
scant 3 tablespoons extra-virgin olive oil
1 clove garlic, finely sliced
1 bay leaf
4 pieces of salmon with skin, each weighing
    6 ounces
salt and pepper to taste
2 pounds potatoes, peeled, boiled and mashed
4 quarters of Middle Eastern preserved lemons,
    flesh discarded and rind finely diced

Cumin and Paprika Oil:

scant 3 tablespoons cumin seeds
scant 3 tablespoons paprika powder
scant 3 tablespoons water
2 cups vegetable oil

Prepare the **cumin and paprika oil** 2 days in advance. Heat the cumin seeds in a small dry pan over low heat, shaking frequently, until the spice smells fragrant. Grind to a powder in a spice or coffee grinder, put it into a bowl and add the paprika and water. Add the oil, stirring to mix, then transfer to a clean screw-top jar and shake vigorously. Keep aside for 2 days, shaking once or twice. This oil can be kept for several months if refrigerated.

Heat the olive oil in a non-stick pan and add the onions. Cook uncovered, stirring constantly, for at least 1 hour. The onions will soften and then slowly darken. Remove the onions from the pan and drain off any excess oil. Store onions in a covered container in the refrigerator; they can be kept for at least 1 week.

Put the peppers, olive oil, garlic and bay leaf into a covered pan. Cook gently for about 45 minutes, turning them from time to time, until tender. Reheat in their oil just before serving.

To finish the dish, season the salmon with salt and pepper. Score the skin in 3 places with a sharp knife, cutting right through the skin to prevent the fish from curling during cooking. Heat a non-stick frying pan until moderately hot. Brush the skin side of the fish with olive oil. Cook with the skin facing up for 1 minute, then turn the fish and cook with the skin touching the pan for 4–6 minutes. The skin should be crisp and brown.

Put some mashed potato in the center of each plate. Surround with pieces of stewed pepper, alternating red and yellow, and top with onion. Put on a piece of fish, skin side up, and scatter over the preserved lemon. Spoon a little cumin oil over the fish and drizzle some among the peppers.

ROAST YABBIES WITH APPLE AND CIDER SAUCE

Stephanie Alexander, Stephanie's, Melbourne

The succulent sweetness of Australia's freshwater crayfish or yabbies is enhanced by a sauce made with cider, apples and butter.

12 yabbies, about 5 ounces each, or small crayfish or slipper lobster
handful of salt
4 teaspoons extra-virgin olive oil
freshly ground black pepper
1 teaspoon fresh thyme leaves

Apple and Cider Sauce:
1 cup dry apple cider
1 cup cider vinegar
4 shallots or 2 pickling onions, finely chopped
1 sprig fresh thyme
1 bay leaf
4 teaspoons extra-virgin olive oil
2 Golden Delicious apples, peeled, cored and cut in $\frac{1}{2}$-inch dice
1 tablespoon cream
10 tablespoons unsalted butter, cut in chunks
scant 3 tablespoons peeled, diced tomato ($\frac{1}{2}$-inch dice)
4 teaspoons freshly chopped parsley
salt to taste

Bring a large pot of salted water to a boil and put in the yabbies for 1 minute. Remove the yabbies and cool in iced water to stop further cooking. Drain well and split each yabby lengthwise. Remove the bony head sack and intestinal thread running down the center. Paint the flesh with olive oil, sprinkle with thyme leaves and grind over black pepper. Arrange on a baking tray and refrigerate until required.

Make the **apple and cider sauce** by bringing the cider, cider vinegar, shallots, thyme and bay leaf to a boil in a stainless steel saucepan. Simmer until most of the liquid has evaporated, then strain.

Heat the olive oil in a non-stick pan and sauté the diced apples until lightly colored. Keep warm.

Reheat the strained sauce and add the cream and heat until it simmers. Whisk in the butter piece by piece fairly quickly, adding the next piece before the previous one has completely melted. Remove from the heat and add the sautéed apples, diced tomato and parsley. Taste for seasoning, adding salt; it may be necessary to add a few drops of cider vinegar to balance the sauce at this point.

To cook the yabbies, put them on the baking tray into a very hot oven preheated to 475°F. Cook for 5 minutes, then transfer the yabbies to warmed plates and spoon the sauce around.

The yabbies can be garnished with some cooked green vegetable such as spinach, or, if it is obtainable, a little samphire (sometimes called sea bean or sea pickle).

MARRON WITH ORANGE AND LEMON ASPEN SAUCE

Andrew Fielke, Red Ochre Grill, Adelaide

Large freshwater crustaceans known as marron are highly prized for their delicate sweet flesh. Lemon aspen, a small wild tropical fruit with a pale lemon color and unique sharp citrus flavor, gives a special dimension to the sauce which accompanies the marron, while the wild vegetable, samphire, adds a dash of intense green. Substitutes for these ingredients are given.

4 marrons or any other small crustaceans such as slipper or flathead lobster, each weighing about 10 ounces
1¹/₂ ounces samphire or 8 green asparagus spears
1 cup fish stock
²/₃ cup white wine
2 large shallots, finely chopped
1¹/₄ ounces lemon aspen fruit, finely chopped, or scant 3 tablespoons lime or lemon juice
1 cup orange juice
1 cup unsalted butter, well chilled
salt and pepper to taste

Opposite:
Ceramic platter by Sudgen Hamilton from The Crafts Council, The Rocks, Sydney.

Split the marrons lengthwise and rinse the stomach cavity clean. Drain and set aside.

Blanch the samphire or asparagus in boiling water until just cooked. Drain, refresh in iced water, drain again and set aside.

Put the fish stock, wine, shallots and lemon aspen fruit or lime juice into a saucepan. Bring to a boil, reduce the heat and simmer until syrupy. Add the orange juice and reduce to approximately 3 tablespoons. Cut 14 tablespoons of the butter into small cubes and gently swirl into the sauce, a few pieces at a time, until all has been incorporated. Taste and adjust seasoning. Strain and keep warm but do not reboil.

Season the marron with salt and pepper. Melt the remaining 2 tablespoons of butter and brush on the marron flesh. Cook over hot charcoal or under a broiler until just cooked through. Quickly reheat the blanched samphire or asparagus with a little butter. Arrange the grilled marron on 4 plates, garnished with the samphire or asparagus and surrounded with the sauce.

CHICKEN BREAST AND PRESERVED LEMON COUSCOUS

Andrew Blake, Blake's, Melbourne

North Africa and Middle Eastern ingredients such as couscous, pomegranate seeds and preserved lemons make an excellent accompaniment to this deceptively simple chicken dish, served with rich pistachio butter.

3 teaspoons olive oil
2 shallots, finely minced
2 cloves garlic, finely minced
$1^1/_2$ cups boiling chicken stock
$1^1/_2$ cups couscous
$^1/_4$ cup fresh pomegranate seeds
$^1/_4$ cup finely diced preserved lemon
4 whole chicken breasts
deep-fried julienne of leeks or parsnips to garnish (optional)

Pistachio Butter:

$^1/_2$ cup unsalted raw pistachio nuts
1 bird's-eye chili
$^1/_4$ cup chopped parsley
11 tablespoons unsalted butter
salt and pepper to taste

Opposite:
Red Coolibah wood platter by Rex Bailey of Golden Canvas Gallery, Balmain, Sydney.

Prepare the **pistachio butter**. Put the pistachio nuts and chili on a baking sheet and roast in a 325°F oven until lightly browned. Allow to cool, then rub off any skins that may be clinging to the nuts. Put the nuts and chili into a food processor and pulse a few times until finely chopped but not mealy. Transfer to a bowl and add the parsley and butter. Mix thoroughly, adding salt and pepper to taste.

Heat the olive oil in a saucepan and gently sauté the shallots and garlic for about 5 minutes. Add the chicken stock and remove from heat. Put the couscous into a bowl and pour over the hot stock. Leave aside for 10 minutes, until the couscous has absorbed all the liquid and swollen. Use a fork to stir in the pomegranate seeds and preserved lemons. Check the seasoning, adding salt and pepper if necessary.

Grill the chicken breasts over charcoal, leaving them slightly pink in the center. Reheat the couscous (a microwave oven is best for this). Divide the couscous among 4 plates, then add a piece of chicken to each and top with a dollop of pistachio butter. Garnish if desired with deep-fried julienne of leeks or parsnips.

STIR-FRIED CHICKEN WITH CONDIMENTS

Allan Koh, Chinois, Melbourne

Seasoned minced pigeon steamed in small bamboo cups is a classic Chinese dish. This version uses chicken, serving it in cups formed by butter lettuce leaves, together with an assortment of crunchy accompaniments. This recipe should serve 4–6 as an appetizer, or 2 as a main course, accompanied by rice and another dish or two.

$^1/_2$ **cup vegetable oil**
10 ounces ground chicken
$^1/_2$ **cup very finely diced onion**
$^1/_2$ **cup very finely diced zucchini**
$^1/_4$ **cup very finely diced red bell pepper**
**3 tablespoons very finely diced yellow bell
  pepper**
2 tablespoons *hoisin* (Chinese barbecue) sauce
4 teaspoons bottled chili garlic sauce
4 teaspoons *sake*
1 teaspoon sugar
$^1/_4$ **teaspoon each salt and white pepper**
**6 butter lettuce leaves, or other cup-shaped
  lettuce**
$^1/_2$ **cup roasted, unsalted peanuts, coarsely crushed**
$^1/_2$ **cup sliced shallots, fried until crisp
  and golden**
$^1/_2$ **cup Chinese sweet mixed pickled vegetables
  (canned or bottled)**

Heat a wok until very hot, then add just over half the oil. Put in the chicken and stir fry until it changes color and is half-cooked. Remove the chicken from the wok and drain in a colander. Reheat the wok, pour in the remaining oil and sauté the onion until transparent, also adding the zucchini and bell peppers. Then put in the chicken, both types of sauce, *sake*, sugar, salt and pepper, tossing to mix well. Cook until all the liquid is absorbed and remove from heat.

Divide the cooked chicken among the lettuce cups and accompany with the peanuts, shallots and pickled vegetables.

ROASTED PHEASANT

Maggie Beer, Pheasant Farm, Nuriootpa, South Australia

Wild game birds are not common in Australia, although they have been raised at Pheasant Farm for the past twenty years. This deceptively simple recipe allows the flavor of the bird to dominate.

2 pheasants, each weighing about 2 pounds
4 teaspoons lemon juice
4 teaspoons finely grated lemon peel
30 juniper berries, bruised
9 sprigs fresh thyme
1 cup *verjus*, or ½ cup dry white wine
1 cup brandy
⅓ cup olive oil
1 large onion
2 stalks celery
2 carrots
4 cups reduced veal stock
sea salt to taste
freshly ground black pepper

Cut the birds along the spine and press your palms firmly on the breastbone to push the pheasants into a butterfly shape. Place the pheasants in a dish and sprinkle with lemon juice, grated lemon peel, juniper berries and thyme. Add ½ cup each of the *verjus* (or ¼ cup of white wine) and brandy and leave to marinate for several hours.

Pour off the marinade and mix with olive oil. Brush all surfaces of the pheasants with this.

Preheat the oven to 475°F. Lay one pheasant at a time in a baking tray; unless you have a large commercial oven it is best to cook one pheasant at a time. Roast for 12–18 minutes, depending upon the heat of the oven. Check after 12 minutes and turn the bird over if not cooked. Return to the oven for a little longer. Rest the cooked bird for at least 20 minutes. The pheasants can either be halved, or remove the legs and breast and carve if you wish. Leave the carved meat, skin side up, sitting in some of the juices from the baking tray to prevent it from drying out.

Roughly chop the onion, celery and carrots. Put into a baking dish lightly greased with olive oil and bake in a 400°F oven for 20–40 minutes, until caramelized. Add the chopped necks and carcasses of the cooked birds. Put in the remaining verjuice and brandy and reduce almost to a syrup, stirring to deglaze the pan. Add the veal stock and simmer vigorously for about 20 minutes to make a rich sauce. Season to taste with salt and pepper. Strain.

In a very hot oven, reheat the carved pheasant in the juices for just 1 minute and serve with the sauce. Roasted root vegetables, such as parsnips or beets, or roasted garlic and onion make a good accompaniment.

FILLET OF VEAL WITH SEA URCHIN AND WASABI BUTTER

Tetsuya Wakuda, Tetsuya's, Sydney

The chef's Japanese origins are evident in the unusual flavoring of the butter which accompanies grilled veal or beef. If fresh sea urchin roe is not available, look for sea urchin paste in a jar in any Japanese food store.

8 veal medallions, or pieces of fillet beef steak, each weighing 2½–3½ ounces
2 teaspoons olive oil
4–5 tablespoons soaked and shredded Japanese *wakame* seaweed, to garnish
4–5 tablespoons Japanese *hijiki* seaweed, simmered in water and soy sauce, to garnish

Sea Urchin and Wasabi Butter:

6½ tablespoons Japanese horseradish (*wasabi*) powder
1 cup unsalted butter, diced
2 ounces fresh sea urchin roe or 1 ounce sea urchin paste
scant 3 tablespoons finely chopped chives
2 teaspoons finely chopped fresh tarragon
½ teaspoon finely chopped fresh thyme
scant 3 tablespoons light soy sauce
2 teaspoons lemon juice
pinch of cayenne pepper

Prepare the **sea urchin and wasabi butter** first by blending the dry *wasabi* powder with sufficient water to make a stiff paste. Put the butter into a food processor and blend until almost white, then add the *wasabi* with all other ingredients and process to mix well. Put the butter onto a foil sheet and roll to make a tube. Store in the freezer until required.

Brush the veal or beef on both sides with the oil and grill or pan fry until medium rare. Place 2 medallions per person on a plate and top with the butter, cut into thick slices. Put the butter-topped meat under a very hot broiler and cook until lightly brown. Garnish with the prepared seaweeds.

Opposite:
Platter by David Hislop from Paddington Bazaar, Sydney.

STUFFED VEAL CUTLETS

Gerda Eilts, The Garden Restaurant, Parmelia Perth Hilton

If you are fortunate enough to be able to obtain smoked tomatoes, these veal cutlets will definitely be out of the ordinary. However, even with regular tomatoes, this easily prepared dish is well worth trying. Serves 6.

6 veal cutlets, each weighing 8 ounces
6 large ripe tomatoes (preferably smoked)
2 tablespoons olive oil
salt and pepper to taste
fresh basil to garnish

Stuffing:

4 ounces finely sliced Parma ham (set aside 4 slices to garnish)
3 medium-sized onions, sliced
14 tablespoons butter
salt and pepper to taste
4 cups fresh white bread crumbs
1 heaped tablespoon finely chopped fresh basil

Prepare the **stuffing** first by frying the onions in a little of the butter until golden brown. Shred the Parma ham and add to the onions together with salt and pepper to taste. Leave to cool. Reserve $3\frac{1}{2}$ tablespoons of the butter and add the remainder, together with the bread crumbs and basil, to the fried onions.

Slit a pocket in the side of each veal cutlet and fill with the stuffing. Close the pocket by pressing the ends together. Heat the reserved butter in a frying pan until very hot and sear the cutlets for about 2 minutes on each side. Transfer to a pan and cook in 350°F oven for 8 minutes.

Peel the tomatoes, cut in half and discard the seeds. Chop the flesh coarsely. Heat the olive oil in a saucepan and fry the slices of parma ham until crisp. Keep the ham aside for garnishing and in the oil remaining in the pan, cook the chopped tomatoes for 2–3 minutes until softened but not mushy. Season to taste with salt and pepper.

Divide the tomatoes among 6 plates and put a cooked veal cutlet on top of each. Garnish with the fried Parma ham and basil and serve with fresh seasonal vegetables and potatoes.

BUFFALO, RAGOUT AND BUSH TOMATO DAMPER

Paul Hoeps, Breezes Restaurant, Cairns Hilton

4 slices buffalo or beef fillet, each weighing
   6 ounces
$1/_2$ cup finely chopped fresh basil
$1/_2$ cup finely chopped fresh oregano
$1^3/_4$ tablespoons finely chopped fresh thyme
$2^2/_3$ cups fresh white bread crumbs
$3/_4$ cup freshly grated Parmesan cheese
$1/_4$ cup white flour
2 eggs beaten with 2 teaspoons water
$1/_4$ cup olive or vegetable oil

Ragout:

2 medium-sized zucchini
1 red and 1 green bell pepper
1 medium-sized onion
$3/_4$ pound eggplant
$1/_4$ cup olive oil
4 cloves garlic, finely chopped
2 cups tomato juice
salt and pepper to taste

Bush Tomato Damper:

2 cups white flour
2 teaspoons baking powder
$1/_2$ teaspoon salt
1 teaspoon sugar
3 teaspoons softened butter
$2/_3$ cup milk
1 ounce bush tomatoes or sun-dried
   tomatoes, soaked to soften

Prepare the **ragout** first by cutting the zucchini, peppers, onion and eggplant (unpeeled) into $1/_4$-inch dice. Heat the oil and gently sauté the garlic for a few seconds. Add the onion and peppers and sauté until onion turns transparent. Add zucchini, sauté for 2–3 minutes, then add eggplant and cook another 2–3 minutes. Add tomato juice, cover and simmer until the mixture is thick and the vegetables tender. Add salt and pepper to taste and set aside.

To make the **bush tomato damper**, sift the flour and baking powder into a bowl. Add all other ingredients and mix. Allow to rest for 30 minutes. Cut into 8 rectangles or circles about $1^1/_4$ inches thick and bake in a 400°F oven for about 20 minutes, until risen and golden.

Cut each buffalo or beef fillet into 2 pieces and flatten to make 8 medallions about $1/_2$ inch thick. Mix the herbs, bread crumbs and cheese. Dip the medallions into the flour, shake off excess, dip into beaten egg and then into the bread crumbs. Heat oil in a pan and fry the medallions on both sides until golden brown; transfer to a 400°F oven for 2–3 minutes. Put some ragout in the center of each of 4 serving plates. Put two medallions on each plate to the side of the ragout and put 2 pieces of damper on the other side. Serve hot, garnished, if desired, with slices of deep-fried turnip.

LAMB CUTLETS, SHEPHERD'S PIE AND RATATOUILLE

Alla Wolf-Tasker, The Lakehouse, Daylesford, Victoria

$1\frac{1}{4}$ pounds lamb leg meat, very finely minced

2 cloves garlic, very finely diced

4 sprigs fresh thyme, very finely chopped

2 sprigs rosemary, very finely chopped

salt and pepper to taste

12–18 lamb cutlets, trimmed

pork caul fat for wrapping the cutlets
   (see below)

1 egg, lightly beaten with 1 teaspoon water to
   make egg wash

shepherd's pie casing (page 138)

shepherd's pie filling (page 138)

Ratatouille:

$\frac{1}{4}$ cup olive oil

2 onions, finely diced

2 cloves garlic, finely minced

4 medium-sized zucchini, finely diced

1 green bell pepper, finely diced

10 ounces unpeeled eggplant, finely diced

10 ounces ripe tomatoes, peeled, deseeded and
   diced

salt and pepper to taste

Combine the minced lamb leg, garlic, herbs, salt and pepper and mix well. Press this around both sides of each lamb cutlet. Gently spread out a piece of the pork caul fat. Cut into pieces large enough to enclose each cutlet and wrap carefully. Refrigerate.

Prepare the **ratatouille** by heating the oil. Gently sauté the onion and garlic until softened. Add the zucchini, pepper and eggplant, and sauté for 2–3 minutes. Add the tomatoes, including any juice which may have come out during dicing. Cover and simmer for 12–15 minutes. Remove cover, cook rapidly for 2 minutes, then season to taste.

Place 6 well-greased circular metal rings at least $2\frac{3}{4}$ inches high and 2 inches in diameter on a greased baking tray. Press some of the shepherd's pie casing across the bottom and up the inside of each ring. Leaving the metal ring in position, fill the center of each potato mold with some of the shepherd's pie filling. Cover with a layer of mashed potato. Brush the top with egg wash and refrigerate until required.

To finish the dish, place the shepherd's pies in a 400°F oven and bake for 15 minutes or until a skewer inserted in the center comes out hot. Seal both sides of the caul-wrapped lamb cutlets in a little oil in a very hot pan, then transfer to a hot oven for 12 minutes for medium-rare meat.

Reheat the ratatouille. Use a spatula to lift each shepherd's pie onto the center of a warm plate. Run a knife around the inside of each mold and lift away the ring. Arrange the cooked cutlets around the pie and garnish with ratatouille. Serves 6.

POT-ROASTED BABY LAMB, ARTICHOKES AND POLENTA

Bill Marchetti, Marchetti's Latin, Melbourne

1 side (half) a baby lamb, or 1 saddle of lamb,
    weighing about 6 pounds
salt and pepper to taste
$1\frac{1}{4}$ cups olive oil
2 cups diced onions
4 teaspoons finely chopped garlic
3 sprigs fresh rosemary
8 anchovy fillets, chopped
$1\frac{2}{3}$ cups dry white wine
juice of 2 lemons
10 whole fresh artichokes
2 cups meat stock
polenta (page 138)

Trim any excess fat from the lamb and discard. Using a heavy knife or cleaver, chop the meat into 2-inch pieces, cutting through the bones and leaving them in. (If you have a cooperative butcher, ask him to do the task for you.) Season the meat with salt and pepper.

Heat 1 cup of the olive oil in a heavy frying pan and add the pieces of meat, spreading out so each piece touches the base of the pan. Cook over medium heat, turning so that the meat is golden brown all over. Transfer the browned lamb to a baking dish.

In the same pan in which the meat was browned, sauté the onions, garlic, rosemary and anchovies until the onions turn light golden. Deglaze with the white wine and pour this over the meat.

Put the lemon juice into a large bowl of cold water. Discard all but the last 4 inches of each artichoke stalk. Discard the hard outer leaves and cut about $\frac{3}{4}$ inch off the top of each artichoke bulb. Cut in half lengthwise and immediately put into the water to prevent them from discoloring. Repeat until all the artichokes are prepared.

Heat the remaining $\frac{1}{4}$ cup olive oil in a large frying pan. Drain the artichokes, pat dry and fry in the hot oil, turning to cook all over. Transfer the artichokes to the baking dish holding the lamb.

Cook in a 350°F oven for about 45 minutes, until the lamb is tender. Keep adding a little of the meat stock and basting the lamb during cooking. When the meat is tender, remove the meat and artichokes and keep warm. Transfer the gravy from the roasting pan to a saucepan and simmer to reduce slightly. Remove any excess fat, check the seasoning and keep warm.

Grill the squares of polenta over a charcoal grill or under a gas or electric broiler until they take color and are thoroughly hot.

To serve, spread some of the lamb sauce on heated dinner plates, add pieces of lamb and artichoke and garnish with the grilled polenta.

LAMB WITH CHICK-PEA CURRY, HARISSA AND NAAN

Bethany Finn, The Grange Brasserie, Adelaide Hilton

2 pounds hogget or lamb loin
Harissa **(page 139)**
2 large red bell peppers
chick–pea curry (page 138)

Naan:
8 cups self-rising flour
2 eggs
1 cup milk
water as needed
scant 3 tablespoons oil
1 teaspoon salt
4 teaspoons black onion seeds or nigella
    (*kalonji*)
4 teaspoons fennel seeds
4 teaspoons white poppy seeds

Prepare the dough for the **naan** by sifting the flour into a large bowl. Whisk the eggs and milk together and add to the flour, mixing in enough water to made a soft dough. Knead in the oil and leave to rest for 3 hours.

Rub the loin of lamb with about 2 tablespoons of the *harissa* and set aside while the oven is heating to 400°F.

Cook the whole peppers under a very hot broiler, turning so that the skin blisters on all sides. Put in a plastic bag for 5–10 minutes (this makes them easier to peel). Peel the skin, discard the seeds and membrane and purée the flesh with the remaining *harissa*. Set aside as a garnish.

To finish the cooking, sear the lamb loin on all sides in a little olive oil in a very hot pan. Transfer it to a baking dish and cook in a 450°F oven for about 10–15 minutes, depending on how well you like the meat cooked.

While the loin is roasting, roll out the *naan* dough, shape into small balls and flatten a little, pulling into a tear-drop shape. Sprinkle the top of each with a mixture of the black onion seeds, fennel seeds and white poppy seeds. Place the *naan* onto a hot baking sheet and bake for 8–10 minutes at 400°F, until puffed and golden brown.

Serve the chick-pea curry in the center of a plate, topped by slices of lamb. Drizzle a little of the pepper and *harissa* purée to one side and serve with the *naan*.

VEAL CUTLETS WITH SHRIMP AND GREEN TEA

Cheong Liew, The Grange Restaurant, Adelaide Hilton

Essentially a Western dish, this "surf and turf" combination of veal and shrimp has a touch of the East in the way the shrimp are prepared with green tea, ginger juice and rice wine. Serves 6.

1 long thin cucumber
6 veal cutlets, about 7 ounces each
salt and freshly ground black pepper to taste
scant 3 tablespoons butter
1 teaspoon *Lung Jian* (green) tea leaves
scant 3 tablespoons hot water
scant 3 tablespoons vegetable oil
2 shallots, finely chopped
1 clove garlic, finely chopped
2 tablespoons Chinese rice wine
4 ounces raw shrimp, peeled
salt to taste
4 teaspoons ginger juice (see helpful hint)
1 teaspoon sugar
¹⁄₂ cup good-quality chicken stock
1¹⁄₂ cups *crème fraiche*, whipped

Cut the cucumber, with the skin still on, into 4 pieces lengthwise. Discard any seeds and cut the flesh into tiny barrel shapes. Freeze until rock hard to bring out maximum flavor.

Season the veal with salt and pepper. Heat the butter in a large frying pan until very hot. Reduce the heat, add the veal cutlets and cook for 5 minutes on each side. Transfer to a plate, cover with foil and keep warm. Do not wash out this frying pan.

Infuse the tea leaves with hot water.

In another frying pan, heat the oil and sauté the shallots and garlic until transparent. Add the cucumber barrels, rice wine and shrimp. Season with salt, ginger juice and sugar and sauté for a few minutes. Add the green tea leaves together with the soaking water. Simmer for 2 minutes over moderate heat.

Deglaze the pan in which the veal was fried by adding the chicken stock and cooking until it is reduced by two-thirds. Add the whipped *crème fraîche* and simmer for 7 minutes. Whisk the sauce.

Place a cutlet on each plate, ladle the cucumber and shrimp mixture over the top and pour over the sauce.

Helpful hint: To make the ginger juice, finely grate a large piece of ginger (about 3 inches) and press in a sieve with the back of a spoon to obtain the juice. If the ginger is a little old and dry, chop and put in a blender with 4 teaspoons of water; blend and strain to obtain juice.

BEEF, DUCK LIVER, BOK CHOY AND BUNYA NUTS

Herbert Franceschini, Victoria's Restaurant, Brisbane Hilton

A true cross-cultural dish, this partners top-quality beef steak with a triangle of puff pastry, Australia's native bunya nuts, Chinese white cabbage and duck liver marinated in a sweet and sour sauce.

8 duck livers
8 whole bunya nuts or chestnuts
1 cup beef stock
salt and pepper to taste
4 triangles of uncooked puff pastry
**   (see below)**
2 tablespoons butter
4 pieces beef fillet, each 6 ounces
2–3 teaspoons vegetable oil
4 baby Chinese white cabbages (*bok choy*),
**   halved lengthwise and blanched in boiling**
**   water until just tender**

Marinade:
½ cup lemon juice
scant 3 tablespoons sugar
2 cloves garlic, crushed
1 red chili, sliced

Combine all **marinade** ingredients in a small saucepan and bring to a boil. Remove from the heat and allow to cool. When the marinade is cool, add the cleaned duck livers and refrigerate for 4–6 hours.

Boil the bunya nuts or chestnuts in plenty of water for 30 minutes or until tender when pierced with a skewer. Drain, and when cool enough to handle, cut in half and remove the bunya nut from the shell, if desired. If using chestnuts, remove from the shell and peel away the fine skin.

Put the beef stock in a small pan and boil until reduced to just 3 tablespoons. Season to taste and add the whole bunya nuts or chestnuts. Reheat gently just before serving.

Buy commercially prepared puff pastry and roll it out until very thin, cutting it into triangles. Bake in a hot oven at 400°F until puffed and golden brown.

While the pastry is baking, drain the marinated duck livers, pat dry and fry in the butter until cooked but still pink inside. Keep warm.

Season the beef with salt and pepper, brush with oil and grill to your liking. Leave the meat to stand in a warm place for 5 minutes before cutting each piece into 3 slices.

Place the beef on serving plates, adding the bunya nuts and sauce, the fried duck liver and the cooked *bok choy*, reheated in a little butter. Garnish with a triangle of puff pastry.

ILLAWARRA PLUM CHEESECAKE WITH RHUBARB SAUCE

Guido van Baelen, Season's Restaurant, Sydney Airport Hilton

Native Illawarra plums, dark red berries from the brown pine, can be replaced by any red or deep purple plums for this cheesecake, which is given extra flavor by the tangy rhubarb sauce. Serves 8.

Crust:

10 ounces bunya nuts or chestnuts, boiled and shelled

1½ cups unsalted macadamia nuts

Opposite:
*Plate by
David Hislop,
Paddington
Bazaar; cutlery
from Ventura
Designs, Lilyfield,
Sydney; vase by
Setsuko Ogishi,
Craft Australia,
David Jones,
Sydney.*

Filling:

1 cup Illawarra plums, or pitted small red or purple plums

1½ cups low-fat ricotta cheese

4 tablespoons apple juice concentrate

4 teaspoons lemon aspen or lime juice

¾ cup apple juice

2 tablespoons powdered gelatin

3 egg whites

pinch of cream of tartar

Rhubarb Sauce:

8 ounces rhubarb (about 2 cups)

¼ cup sugar

3 tablespoons maple syrup

1 cup water

To prepare the **crust**, process the bunya nuts or chestnuts with the macadamia nuts to form fine crumbs. Press into a 10-inch pie plate greased with a little butter and bake in a 350°F oven for about 25 minutes or until light brown.

While the crust is cooking, make the **filling**. Blend the plums, ricotta cheese, apple juice concentrate and lemon aspen juice together until smooth. Put the apple juice in a small saucepan and sprinkle the gelatin over. Put over low heat and stir until the gelatin has dissolved. Add to the plum mixture. Beat the egg whites briefly, then add the cream of tartar and continue beating until stiff. Fold into the plum mixture, pour over the cooked crust and refrigerate.

To make the **rhubarb sauce**, peel the rhubarb and cut into 2-inch lengths. Blanch in a saucepan of boiling water for 2 minutes, then drain. Combine sugar, maple syrup and water in a saucepan and boil until it forms a syrup and starts to change color. Add the rhubarb, lower the heat and cook gently for about 20 minutes, stirring constantly to prevent the mixture from sticking. Allow to cool.

To serve, spread some of the rhubarb sauce over a plate, making a decoration by incorporating some cream if desired. Place a slice of the cheesecake over the sauce and serve with more of the rhubarb sauce drizzled over the top.

BAKLAVA OF DRIED FRUITS WITH MINT SYRUP

Dietmar Sawyere, Forty One Restaurant, Sydney

Inspired by the Greek baklava, which normally contains crushed nuts between layers of flaky filo pastry, this recipe also incorporates some of the dried fruits for which Australia is justifiably renowned.

1 cup coarsely chopped mixed dried fruit (apricots, cherries and pears)
2 cups raw unsalted pistachios
½ cup ground hazelnuts
½ cup sugar
1 teaspoon ground cinnamon
5 tablespoons plus 1 teaspoon Grand Marnier
9 sheets filo pastry
10–14 tablespoons unsalted butter, melted
⅓ cup diced dried fruit (same mixture as above)
clotted cream or ice cream to accompany

Mint Syrup:
½ cup superfine sugar
½ cup water
2 sprigs mint

Blend the dried fruit, pistachios, hazelnuts, sugar, cinnamon and Grand Marnier in a food processor to achieve a coarse mixture. Do not over blend; there should be some texture to the filling.

Place a sheet of filo pastry on a large wooden board or tabletop and brush with some of the melted butter. Place a second sheet on top and brush again. Repeat with a third sheet of pastry.

Spoon one-third of the filling onto the pastry and spread out to within ¾ inch of the edge. Starting at one end, roll up tightly and place on a well-buttered baking sheet. Brush with more melted butter.

Repeat this process with the remaining filo pastry, so you have a total of three filled rolls. Refrigerate the rolls for 30 minutes. Bake in a 400°F oven for 10–15 minutes until golden brown.

While the pastry is baking, prepare the **mint syrup**. Combine the sugar, water and mint in a pan, bring to a boil and simmer for 2 minutes.

When the baklava rolls are golden, remove from the oven, place on a cooling rack over a plate and spoon over a little of the syrup while the baklava is still warm. Add the diced dried fruit to the remaining syrup and bring to a boil. Remove from heat and keep aside.

To serve, slice the baklava (preferably while still warm) and arrange on 4 serving plates. Spoon over some of the syrup with diced fruits and serve either with clotted cream or ice cream. Grand Marnier or Poire William ice cream go particularly well with the baklava.

PUMPKIN SCONES AND BANANA BREAD

Werner Kimmeringer, Cliveden Room, Melbourne Hilton

PUMPKIN SCONES

$^1/_2$ cup granulated sugar
$^1/_2$ cup water
1 cup cooked pumpkin, cut in $^1/_2$-inch dice
$^1/_4$ cup superfine sugar
2 tablespoons softened butter
$1^1/_2$ cups cooked, mashed winter squash
   (preferably butternut variety)
1 egg
$2^1/_2$ cups self-rising flour
pinch of salt
$^1/_2$ teaspoon ground cinnamon
$^1/_4$ teaspoon freshly grated nutmeg
$^1/_4$–$^1/_2$ cup milk (see below)

Combine the granulated sugar and water together in a small saucepan and simmer, stirring from time to time, until a syrup forms. Cool and add the diced pumpkin. Leave to marinate for a minimum of 8 hours; the pumpkin can be left for up to 3 days.

Beat the superfine sugar and butter together, then add the mashed squash and mix well. Beat in the egg. Sift the flour, salt, cinnamon and nutmeg into the pumpkin mixture, then add $^1/_4$ cup of milk. If necessary, add more milk to make a soft but not sticky dough; the amount of milk required will depend on the dryness of the squash. Drain the soaked diced pumpkin and add to the dough, turning the mixture out onto a floured surface. Knead lightly, then pat out to a thickness of $^3/_4$ inch. Cut into rectangles or use a floured cookie cutter to cut 2-inch diameter circles.

Place the scones on a greased tray and bake in a 400°F oven for 12–15 minutes, until risen and golden brown. Serve while still warm with fresh whipped cream.

BANANA BREAD

1 cup mashed ripe bananas
$1^1/_4$ cups brown sugar
3 eggs, lightly beaten
pinch salt
$^1/_2$ cup milk
$^1/_3$ cup vegetable oil
$2^1/_2$ cups white flour
1 teaspoon baking soda
$1^1/_2$ teaspoons baking powder

Mix the bananas, brown sugar and eggs together. Add the salt to the banana mixture, then stir in the milk. Add the oil and continue stirring.

Sift the flour, baking soda and baking powder together, then add to the banana mixture. Blend together in a cake mixer for 10 minutes; this is important to ensure that the banana bread will be light. Pour into a greased loaf pan 12 inches x 3 inches. Bake at 325°F for 2 hours.

CANNOLI ALLA SICILIANA

Bill Marchetti, Marchetti's Latin, Melbourne

If you are unable to find the metal tubes for making cannoli in a kitchen shop, use 4-inch lengths of wooden dowels about ¾ inch in diameter. This recipe makes about 20 cannoli.

6 cups white flour
11 tablespoons unsalted butter, melted
4 whole eggs
4 additional egg yolks
1 cup dry Marsala
pinch of salt
4 cups olive oil
1 pound pork lard (optional)
confectioner's sugar

Ricotta Filling:
1¼ pounds ricotta cheese
4 ounces mascarpone
5 ounces mixed glacé fruits, finely diced
about ½ cup Maraschino liqueur
4 tablespoons superfine sugar, or more to taste

Orange Sauce:
4 cups freshly squeezed orange juice
1 cup superfine sugar
½ cup Grand Marnier
3 teaspoons cornstarch mixed with a little cold water

Opposite:
Cutlery and blue plate from Villeroy & Boch, French's Forest, Sydney; glass platter from David Hislop, Paddington Bazaar, Sydney.

Prepare the cannoli first. Put the flour into the bowl of an electric mixer, make a well in the middle and pour in the melted butter, 2 whole eggs (reserving 2 for later use) and 4 egg yolks. Add the Marsala and salt and mix the dough on medium speed for about 5 minutes, until the dough is elastic. Put dough into a covered bowl and refrigerate for 2 hours to firm.

To make the **orange sauce**, combine the juice, sugar and Grand Marnier in a saucepan and simmer over moderate heat until reduced to about half. Mix in the cornstarch and water and cook, stirring, until the sauce thickens and clears. Strain and cool.

Mix the **ricotta filling** by combining the ricotta, mascarpone and fruits in a bowl. Add Maraschino and sugar to taste and set aside.

When the cannoli dough has rested for 2 hours, roll it out in a pasta machine until very thin. Cut into squares of 3½ inches. Put a cannoli rod diagonally across each square of dough and roll up, so that the diagonal points meet in the middle. Lightly beat the 2 remaining eggs and brush the edges of each cannoli with this to seal.

Heat the olive oil and pork lard together (the lard improves the texture). Fry the cannoli in the hot oil until light golden in color. Remove, drain, and when cool, pull out the tubes or dowels.

Use a piping bag to fill each cooled cannoli with the ricotta filling. Dust with confectioner's sugar and serve with the orange sauce.

PAVLOVA WITH SEASONAL FRUITS

Marieke Brugman, Howqua Dale Gourmet Retreat, Mansfield, Victoria

This classic dessert, named after a famous ballerina, is popular in both Australia and New Zealand.

12 egg whites
3 cups superfine sugar
4 teaspoons cornstarch
1 teaspoon white vinegar
winter or spring fruits: a mixture of peeled and diced papaya, rock melon, cantaloupe, pineapple and mango
summer or autumn fruits: raspberries, strawberries, loganberries, boysenberries or blueberries
1–2 teaspoons lime or lemon juice
superfine sugar to taste

Crème Chantilly:

1¼ cups whipping cream
1 teaspoon pure vanilla extract
4 tablespoons superfine sugar
10 large strawberries, puréed

Passion-fruit Caramel:

1 cup sugar
4 tablespoons water
pulp from 6–8 passion-fruit

Line two baking sheets with parchment paper. Using a saucer as a guide, draw 6 circles about 3–4 inches in diameter on each piece of baking paper, to make 12 mini-pavlovas. Set aside.

In a food mixer with a balloon whisk attachment, beat the egg whites until they start to mount in volume. Add the vinegar and continue beating until stiff. Sift over the cornstarch, add 1½ cups of sugar and beat again until very stiff and glossy. Keep the beaters running and very quickly incorporate the remaining 1½ cups of sugar, a little at a time.

Put the mixture into a large piping bag fitted with a plain ½-inch nozzle. Following the circles drawn on the paper, pipe the mixture into neat disks about 2½–3 inches high. Bake the pavlovas in a 200°F oven for 1¼–1½ hours, until the exterior is very crisp.

Prepare either summer or winter fruits according to season. Toss with a little lemon juice and sugar.

Make the **passion-fruit caramel** by dissolving the sugar in water. Bring to a boil and cook until it turns a dark mahogany color. Immediately add the passion-fruit pulp and put back over low heat to dissolve the caramel.

Whip together the cream, vanilla and sugar to make the ***crème chantilly***, adding the puréed strawberries to one-third of the cream. To serve, put the pavlovas in the center of a plate and surround with mixed fruit. At the last minute, spread the strawberry *crème chantilly* over the top of the pavlovas, add the passion-fruit caramel and serve the remaining *crème chantilly* separately. Serves 12.

LEMON MYRTLE BAVAROIS WITH ROSELLA FLOWER JELLY

Andrew Fielke, Red Ochre Grill, Adelaide

macadamia or any other nut oil for brushing
the molds
5 teaspoons powdered gelatin
scant $^2/_3$ cup warm water
$1^2/_3$ cups whipping cream
$1^3/_4$ cups milk
1 cup sugar
10 lemon myrtle leaves, or 5–6 kaffir lime
leaves, finely shredded
5 egg yolks

Rosella Flower Jelly:

10 ounces rosella flowers, or 1 cup puréed
raspberry and rhubarb
1 cup sugar
3 tablespoons lemon juice
2 cups water
5 teaspoons powdered gelatin
scant $^2/_3$ cup warm water

Use the oil to brush 10–12 ring molds, each about $2^1/_2$ inches in diameter and 4 inches high. Alternatively, use small soufflé or ramekin dishes.

Sprinkle the gelatin over warm water and leave until it softens and swells. Whip the cream to soft peaks and refrigerate.

Bring the milk, sugar and lemon myrtle leaves to a boil. Remove the pan from the heat immediately and stand for 10 minutes.

Whisk the egg yolks and pour in the warm milk, whisking fast all the time. Put the pan containing the mixture over a larger saucepan containing rapidly boiling water. Continue whisking until a custard forms.

Remove from the heat and add the gelatin. Mix well, pour through a fine sieve into a bowl and stand it in iced water. Stir continuously until the mixture cools and just begins to thicken. Quickly fold in the whipped cream and pour into the oiled molds or soufflé dishes, leaving about $^1/_2$ inch at the top for the jelly to be added. Keep in the refrigerator.

Prepare the rosella flower jelly by chopping the flower petals finely. Put the rosellas or raspberry and rhubarb purée in a pan with 2 cups water, sugar and lemon juice. Bring to a boil, lower the heat and simmer for 5 minutes, skimming the surface frequently. Pour the mixture through a fine sieve, measure 2 cups and mix in the gelatin, which has first been softened in $^2/_3$ cup water.

Allow the jelly mixture to cool to room temperature, then pour a layer over the top of the bavarois. Leave to set in the refrigerator.

LEMON CURD TART WITH CREAM

Bethany Finn, The Grange Brasserie, Adelaide Hilton

Opposite:
*Fork from
Villeroy & Boch,
French's Forest,
Sydney; placemat
from Prima Cosa,
Balmain, Sydney.*

This rich egg custard with a tangy lemon flavor is ideally accompanied by fresh Kangaroo Island cream, pure dairy cream from South Australia.

9 eggs
2 cups sugar
1 teaspoon finely grated lemon rind
1 cup lemon juice, strained
1 vanilla bean
1 cup Kangaroo Island or other fresh cream
confectioner's sugar to garnish
additional heavy cream to garnish

Pastry:

14 tablespoons butter
$\frac{1}{2}$ cup sugar
pinch of salt
1 egg
$2\frac{3}{4}$ cups white flour

Prepare the **pastry** first by mixing butter, sugar and salt until well combined. Add the egg and mix again, then add the flour and knead until well combined. Take care not to overknead or the pastry will become too elastic. Refrigerate for 1 hour, then roll out into a very thin circle. Thoroughly grease the bottom and sides of a 10-inch pie plate with a removable base and carefully press in the circle of pastry so that it covers the bottom and the sides. Trim the top edge with a sharp knife. Do not let any cracks or holes form in the pastry, which must come right up the the top of the pie plate.

Refrigerate pastry for 15 minutes. Put a circle of aluminum foil into the center and coming up the sides of the pastry and fill with beans or rice. Bake for 15 minutes in a 350°F oven.

While the pastry is baking, make the filling by whisking together the eggs and sugar to mix well, but take care to avoid whipping any air into the eggs. Add the lemon rind and juice and stir to mix. Cut the vanilla bean in half and scrape out the seeds. Put these into the egg mixture and finally stir in the 1 cup of cream.

When the pastry has been baked for 15 minutes, remove from the oven and carefully pour in the lemon filling. Reduce the heat to 300°F and bake for 1 hour. By this time, the filling should be just set but still somewhat soft, like a jelly. Check by gently tapping the tin; if the center is still runny, bake for another 5–10 minutes and test again.

When the tart is baked, cool and then refrigerate for 1 hour. Remove the base from the pie plate and slide the tart onto a serving plate. Dust with confectioner's sugar to make an even layer on the top of the tart and place under a hot grill for a few moments until it becomes brown and caramelized. Serve with plenty of fresh cream.

STEAMED MACADAMIA AND BANANA PUDDING

Herbert Franceschini, Victoria's Restaurant, Brisbane Hilton

7 tablespoons butter
9$\frac{1}{2}$ tablespoons sugar
4 eggs, separated
a few drops of vanilla extract
pinch of salt
4 ounces vanilla sponge cake (2 pieces), dried and crumbled
$\frac{3}{4}$ cup lightly toasted unsalted macadamia nuts, chopped
$\frac{1}{2}$ cup mashed banana
$\frac{1}{2}$ cup cream
1 teaspoon lemon rind
scant 3 tablespoons lemon juice

Caramel Sauce:

1 cup sugar
3 tablespoons hot water
1 cup cream

Chocolate Sauce:

$\frac{1}{2}$ cup cream
$\frac{1}{2}$ cup milk
4 teaspoons honey
5 ounces dark chocolate, grated

Sugar Bark:

$\frac{1}{2}$ cup superfine sugar
1 teaspoon instant coffee granules

To make the **sugar bark**, put sugar into a dry heavy pan and cook, without any water, over very low heat until golden brown. Sprinkle coffee granules on a large sheet of paper and pour over the browned sugar, spreading it with the back of a spoon to make a thin layer. Leave to set.

Prepare the **caramel sauce** by putting the sugar and water into a pan and cooking until it turns golden brown. Heat the cream in a separate pan. When the sugar has caramelized, stir in the boiling cream. Transfer to a jug and leave to cool.

To make the **chocolate sauce**, bring the cream, milk and honey to a boil, then whisk in the grated chocolate until it dissolves. Set aside.

Prepare the pudding by whisking the butter with $\frac{1}{4}$ cup of the sugar until fluffy. Whisk in the egg yolks, 1 at a time. In a separate bowl, whip the egg whites with the remaining sugar and salt until stiff. Fold one-third of this into the sugar and butter mixture, then fold in the remaining egg white. Fold in the cake crumbs, nuts and mashed banana, then fold in cream, lemon rind and juice.

Grease 4 timbales and sprinkle with a little additional sugar. Put in the pudding mixture and place the timbales into a baking dish with water to come halfway up the sides. Cover timbales with foil and bake at 350°F for 1 hour.

Unmold and serve surrounded by the two sauces. Break the sugar bark with your hands into large pieces and use as a garnish.

POT-ROASTED QUINCES

Maggie Beer, Pheasant Farm, Nuriootpa, South Australia

Quinces, popular in the past, seem to have almost disappeared from today's fruit shops. Maggie Beer is so enthusiastic about them that she has established a quince orchard and is trying to share her love of this fruit. Quinces have the remarkable property of turning from a pale yellow to gold and through to a deep red color during long slow cooking, making them as decorative as they are delicious. This dish is best attempted at the beginning of the season, when the quinces hold their shape better.

Opposite:
Plate, espresso cups and napkin ring by Jan Hannah, Balmain Market, Sydney.

6 whole quinces
6 cups water
4 cups sugar
4 tablespoons lemon juice

Rub the down off the skin of the quinces and wash the fruit well, but do not peel. Try to keep the leaves on the stem if the fruit was obtained with them.

Choose a heavy-bottomed pan with a tightly fitting lid. Add water and sugar and bring to a boil, then put in the whole quinces, cover the pan and simmer for up to 3 hours. It is important to turn the quinces 2 or 3 times during cooking so that the rich red color flows right through to the core of the fruit. Add the lemon juice about 20 minutes before the end of cooking time to remove excess sweetness.

Turn the temperature down if the juices seem in danger of burning, using a simmering mat or heat diffuser if necessary towards the final stage of cooking. The liquid will reduce to a thick red syrup. Serve the quinces with a little of the syrup and *crème anglaise* (rich custard).

Supplementary Recipes

These recipes are required for some of the main dishes, as indicated by the page numbers on each supplementary recipe

Quatre Épices • *see page 42*

3 teaspoons whole allspice
$\frac{1}{2}$ nutmeg, smashed
2 teaspoons whole cloves
$\frac{3}{4}$ inch cinnamon stick

Combine the whole spices in a spice grinder or coffee mill and blend until finely powdered. Strain.

Rabbit Stock • *see page 42*

rabbit bones (see page 42)
1 medium-sized onion, sliced
1 clove garlic, bruised
1 small carrot, diced
1 stalk celery, sliced
$\frac{2}{3}$ cup white wine
1 teaspoon salt
sprig of fresh thyme
parsley stalk and leaves
1 bay leaf

Combine the rabbit bones with all stock ingredients in a pan. Add water to cover. Bring to a boil, cover and simmer for 3 hours. Strain and reserve.

Tea-Smoking Mixture • *see page 56*

4 teaspoons Chinese black oolong tea leaves
4 teaspoons Chinese jasmine tea leaves
zest of 1 orange
2 pieces dried tangerine peel, broken

scant 3 tablespoons raw fragrant long-grain ("jasmine") rice
scant 3 tablespoons brown sugar
3 whole star anise
2 teaspoons Sichuan peppercorns
3 pieces cassia bark

Combine all ingredients and use as directed.

Sweet and Sour Dressing • *see page 56*

$\frac{1}{2}$ cup vegetable oil
pinch of dried hot red pepper flakes
2 small cloves garlic, finely sliced
$\frac{1}{4}$ cup light soy sauce
$\frac{1}{2}$ cup cider vinegar
$\frac{2}{3}$ cup sugar syrup, made from equal parts of sugar and water

Gently heat the oil together with red pepper flakes and garlic over low heat until the garlic is golden; take great care not to burn the garlic or it will be bitter. Add all other dressing ingredients and bring to a boil. Remove from the heat and allow to cool.

Servings

Unless otherwise stated, the recipes are designed to serve 4 persons.

Dressing for Lentil Salad • see page 60

4 teaspoons reduced chicken stock
$\frac{1}{2}$ cup heavy cream
scant $\frac{1}{2}$ cup olive oil
***verjus* or lemon juice to taste**
salt and pepper to taste

Prepare the dressing by mixing the chicken stock and cream, slowly working in the oil. Acidulate to taste with *verjus* or lemon juice and season well with salt and pepper.

Ravioli Filling • see page 64

2 teaspoons olive oil
$\frac{1}{4}$ pound finely diced mixed vegetables (carrot, leek and celery)(about $\frac{1}{3}$ cup each)
meat from bodies and claws of 8 yabbies or 8 shrimp, cut in large cubes
salt and pepper to taste
$\frac{1}{4}$ pound fresh salmon, finely chopped

Heat the oil in pan and sauté the vegetables and yabby meat for just 30 seconds. Season to taste with salt and pepper and allow to cool before mixing in the salmon.

Ravioli Dough • see page 64

2 cups white flour
3 whole eggs
1 additional egg yolk
4 teaspoons olive oil
4 teaspoons water
Salt and white pepper to taste
1 teaspoon chopped parsley

Mix all the ingredients together in a food processor or combine quickly by hand. Do not overwork the dough; otherwise, it will become tough. Cover with plastic until needed.

Béchamel Sauce • see page 68

1 cup milk
1 bay leaf
a little freshly grated nutmeg
scant 3 tablespoons butter
scant 3 tablespoons white flour
salt and pepper to taste

Bring the milk to a boil together with the bay leaf and nutmeg. Remove the pan from the heat. In a separate saucepan, melt the butter over low heat and stir in the flour, mixing until smooth. Add the heated milk and whisk well. Season with salt and pepper and cook over low heat, stirring continuously, for 10 minutes. Transfer the béchamel sauce to a bowl and cover the surface with a piece of buttered waxed paper to prevent a skin from forming.

Pasta Dough • see page 68

$5\frac{1}{2}$ cups white bread flour
5 eggs, beaten
4 teaspoons olive oil
$\frac{1}{2}$ teaspoon salt

Put the flour into a large bowl, make a well in the center and add the eggs, oil and salt, stirring in gradually. Knead the dough until smooth, then rest for 15 minutes. Roll out the dough into several very thin sheets, sprinkling them with flour and keeping covered with a cloth those you are not working with.

Butter Sauce • see page 68

2 cups fish stock
$^{1}/_{2}$ cup butter
10 tablespoons salted butter, cut into small
    cubes and frozen
scant 3 tablespoons finely chopped chives
a little freshly ground black pepper

Put the fish stock into a saucepan, bring to a boil and cook over high heat until reduced to about $^{1}/_{2}$ cup. Add the frozen butter piece by piece, whisking in to form a sauce. Keep in a warm place.

Saffron Custard • see page 74

1 pint cream (35% fat content)
1 teaspoon saffron threads
2 large or 3 small whole eggs
3 additional egg yolks
salt and white pepper to taste
dash of Tabasco sauce

Make the custard by heating the cream and saffron until almost boiling. Remove from the heat and leave to infuse for 1 hour, stirring from time to time to prevent a skin from forming on top. Lightly whisk the cream with the whole eggs and egg yolks and season with salt, pepper and Tabasco. Do not whisk the mixture too much and create a foam.

Bush Tomato Salsa • see page 76

$^{1}/_{4}$ cup olive oil
1 medium-sized onion, diced
$2^{1}/_{2}$ tablespoons curry powder
1 teaspoon cayenne powder
salt and pepper to taste
1 pound bush tomatoes or sun-dried tomatoes,
    soaked to soften

2$^{1}/_{2}$ cups sugar
1 cup red wine vinegar
salt and pepper to taste

Heat the oil and sauté the onion, curry powder and cayenne until the onion softens. Add the tomatoes, sugar and vinegar and simmer, uncovered, until the tomatoes break up and the sauce thickens. Season to taste with salt and pepper.

Shrimp Mousse • see page 80

$^{3}/_{4}$ pound peeled raw shrimp
2 egg whites
3 teaspoons lemon juice
pinch sea salt
pinch of freshly ground white pepper
scant 1$^{1}/_{4}$ cups crème fraîche

Chop the shrimp meat into small chunks. Put this into a food processor with the egg whites, lemon juice, salt and pepper. Process until the mixture becomes a fine paste, then add the crème fraîche and blend only just until the mixture adheres; too much processing will cause the mousse to split and fall apart during cooking. The shrimp mousse should be quite firm in texture.

Shrimp Sauce • see page 80

$^{3}/_{4}$ pound fresh shrimp heads
3 tablespoons Chinese *shaoxing* wine
3 tablespoons vegetable oil
1 onion, finely chopped
3 cloves garlic, finely chopped
1 heaped tablespoon finely chopped ginger root
1 red or green bird's-eye chili, finely chopped
2 kaffir lime leaves, very finely chopped
1 stalk lemon grass, very finely chopped

1 whole star anise
1 teaspoon coriander seeds
1 teaspoon Sichuan peppercorns
½ teaspoon fennel seeds
5 ripe tomatoes, roasted in a pan in a hot oven for 20–25 minutes until slightly blackened and soft
3 cups fish stock
1 cup crème fraîche
fish sauce to taste
lime juice to taste

Sear shrimp heads in a hot wok until they begin to turn pink. Add the *shaoxing* wine, stir to deglaze the pan and remove from heat. Heat oil in a saucepan and sauté the onion, garlic, ginger, chili, lime leaves and lemon grass until the onion turns transparent. Add the spices and stir fry for a couple of minutes. Add the shrimp heads and their juices, the roasted tomatoes and any juice from the roasting pan. Put in the fish stock and stir to combine all ingredients.

Bring to a boil, then reduce to a medium simmer and cook for 2 hours, skimming the surface regularly. Pour the stock through a fine mesh sieve, discard the solids and put the strained stock into a clean pan. Bring back to a boil and add the crème fraîche. Let it return to a boil and stir to incorporate the cream. Simmer for 15 minutes to allow the sauce to thicken, then add fish sauce and lime juice, a drop at a time, tasting until the sauce is seasoned to your taste. Set aside, reheating just before serving.

Bush Tomato Chutney • see page 82

10 tablespoons treacle or golden syrup (or substitute dark corn syrup)
½ cup finely chopped shallots
2½ tablespoons finely chopped garlic
2½ tablespoons finely chopped ginger root
5 medium-sized ripe tomatoes, peeled and seeds discarded
1 cup malt vinegar
½ cup vegetable oil
2½ tablespoons black mustard seeds
1 cinnamon stick
4 teaspoons salt
½ pound dried bush tomatoes or sun-dried tomatoes, soaked to soften
1 red and 1 green bird's-eye chili, deseeded and finely chopped
1 whole bunch of cilantro, leaves and roots washed and chopped

Heat the treacle or golden syrup gently in a pan, then add the shallots, garlic, ginger and tomatoes and cook for 30 seconds. Add the vinegar and stir to mix well. Heat the oil in a separate small saucepan, add the mustard seeds and cover the pan. When the mustard seeds finish popping, transfer them to the syrup mix and add all other ingredients. Simmer the chutney for 15 minutes, then transfer to a clean jar. Cool and cover.

Lemon Butter Sauce • see page 82

½ cup butter
¼ cup finely chopped shallots
1 teaspoon crushed white peppercorns
3 tablespoons lemon juice
4 teaspoons white wine vinegar
a touch of white wine
1 cup strong fish stock
4 teaspoons light cream
salt and pepper to taste

Heat the butter in a saucepan, sauté the shallots and peppercorns until the shallots turn transparent, then add the lemon juice and vinegar. Stir and reduce until the mixture is almost dry, then add a touch of white wine and repeat the action. Add fish stock and simmer, uncovered, until reduced by half. Strain the sauce, put back into a clean pan, then add the cream and butter, stirring over low heat for 15 minutes. Season well with salt and pepper. Do not bring the sauce back to a boil as it will separate.

Shepherd's Pie Casing • see page 106

1½–2 cups dry mashed potato
1 teaspoon olive oil
1 egg, lightly beaten
salt and pepper to taste

Beat the mashed potato with a wooden spoon until perfectly smooth. Add oil, egg and seasoning and beat until well incorporated and smooth.

Shepherd's Pie Filling • see page 106

3 large lamb shanks
2 teaspoons butter
2 teaspoons olive oil
½ stalk celery, chopped
½ onion, chopped
½ carrot, chopped
2 cloves garlic
1 bay leaf
1 sprig thyme
2–3 cups lamb stock
1 cup dry white wine

Heat the butter and oil in a heavy saucepan or casserole of sufficient size to just hold the lamb shanks. Brown the shanks on all sides, add the vegetables, herbs, stock and wine to just cover the shanks. Bring to a boil, cover, and simmer gently for 1–1½ hours, until the meat is sufficiently tender to come off the bone. Remove the meat. Strain and cool the stock and adjust seasoning. Cut the meat into chunks, put back in the stock and refrigerate until required.

Polenta • see page 108

8 cups water
4 teaspoons olive oil
3 tablespoons butter
3¼ cups polenta
salt to taste
1¼ cups grated fontina or gruyère cheese

Bring the water to a boil with the oil and butter. When it is bubbling, slowly pour in the polenta, stirring constantly so that no lumps form. When the mixture comes back to a boil, lower the heat, add the salt and cook, stirring constantly, for 45 minutes. If you do not stir the mixture, it will stick to the bottom of the pan. When the polenta is cooked, add the cheese and stir until thoroughly melted. Check the seasoning and pour out into a rectangular container to a depth of about ¾ inch. Cool for at least 1 hour before cutting into 4-inch squares. The polenta will keep up to 5 days refrigerated.

Chick-pea Curry • see page 110

2 cups chick-peas (garbanzos), soaked overnight
scant 3 tablespoons vegetable oil
2 onions, coarsely chopped
6 cloves garlic, finely chopped
1 inch ginger root, finely chopped
1 teaspoon turmeric powder

4 teaspoons cumin seeds, toasted and ground
1½ cups coconut milk
fresh cilantro leaves to garnish

Soak the chick-peas in cold water overnight. The following day, drain, simmer in fresh water until almost tender and drain again. Heat the oil and sauté the onion, garlic and ginger until transparent and fragrant, then sprinkle in the turmeric and cumin and sauté for a few seconds. Stir in the coconut milk, then add the chick-peas and simmer for about 15 minutes, until the chick-peas are soft. The curry can be kept aside and reheated gently immediately before serving.

Harissa • see page 110

4–6 cloves garlic
4 teaspoons dried mint
4 teaspoons chopped fresh mint
4 teaspoons freshly ground coriander seeds or
    coriander powder
4 tablespoons fresh cilantro leaves
4 teaspoons salt
2 teaspoons freshly ground caraway seeds
2 or more chilies (deseeded if you don't want
    recipe to be too hot)
⅔ cup olive oil

Combine all ingredients and blend or process until you have a thick paste. Store in a covered jar.

Appendix: Contributors

Stephanie Alexander has won numerous personal awards and accolades for Stephanie's, owned by her and her partner, Dur-é Dara. Listed as Australia's top restaurant and one of the ten best in the world in *Courvoisier's Book of the Best*, Stephanie's opened in Melbourne in 1976. Ms Alexander has led the way in encouraging Australian suppliers to produce world-class raw items, and has written four books for food lovers, including *Stephanie's Australia*.

Guido van Baelen trained in his native Belgium, then worked in Algeria, South Africa and London. In 1988 he was appointed Executive Sous Chef at Cairns Hilton and for the past 6 years he has been Executive Chef at the Sydney Airport Hilton. He is well known for his creative cooking classes and is an active member of La Chaine des Rotisseurs.

Tony Baker is an Adelaide-based writer, journalist and author, who was born in England and went to Australia in the late 1960s because he had heard the wine was good and cheap. As well as being a daily newspaper editor and columnist, he has written about the Australian good life for almost 20 years for numerous publications.

Maggie Beer, regarded by many as the pioneer of Australian regional cuisines and as "one of the great country cooks of all time," runs the famous Pheasant Farm restaurant at the game farm owned by herself and husband Colin in the Barossa Valley of South Australia.

Beh Kim Un, originally from Penang in Malaysia, grew up surrounded by good food. Shortly after graduating in Industrial Chemistry in Melbourne in 1977, he moved out of the laboratory into the kitchen. His imaginative interpretation of Asian cuisine is given exposure in three Melbourne restaurants, Monsoon, The Isthmus of Kra and Shakahari. He frequently demonstrates in leading cooking schools.

Andrew Blake began working in Melbourne in 1980 at the most famous restaurant of the day, Fanny's, then worked in top Sydney restaurants from 1985 to 1989. Returning to Melbourne, he introduced his signature style to Cafe Kanis, then went on to open Blake's in 1992. He describes his food as "fresh and modern" and is known for his eclectic style.

Marieke Brugman was born in Melbourne to Dutch parents. She left Australia for Europe in 1969, returning to Australia to study Fine Arts. In 1977 she established the Howqua Dale Gourmet Retreat with Sarah Stegley. She later opened the Howqua Dale Cooking School, Australia's only residential participatory program. She has been in the forefront of the movement to establish fine dining in Australia's rural areas.

Rita Erlich is a senior journalist with the Melbourne newspaper, *The Age*, with a special interest in food and wine. She is the author of a number of books on food and cooking, and the co-editor of the best selling and highly respected annual guide to Victoria's restaurants, *The Age Good Food Guide*.

Cheong Liew grew up in multiracial Malaysia. He came to study in Australia in 1970 and later worked in a variety of European and Asian restaurants in both Melbourne and Adelaide. He became chef at Adelaide Hilton's Grange Restaurant in 1995. Often credited as the first chef in Australia to fully exploit a fusion of several Asian and Western styles, Cheong Liew believes this approach to cooking is only natural in multicultural Australia.

Gerda Eilts began her training in her native Germany, then worked in London and South Africa before joining the Hilton International Australia in 1985. She became Executive Sous Chef at Brisbane Hilton in 1990, and Executive Chef at Parmelia Perth Hilton in 1995. One of the new breed of chefs creating a contemporary Australian cuisine, Gerda is also among the few to have earned a degree as a Master Chef.

Andrew Fielke was trained as a cook in his native Adelaide before working in Europe for a few years. Upon returning to Australia, he learned of the budding movement to gather and use wild native ingredients and started the Red Ochre Grill in 1992 to develop and feature indigenous Australian food. A branch of this restaurant opened in Cairns in 1994. Fielke is also involved in the gathering, growing and production of native foods.

Bethany Finn, Executive Chef of the Adelaide Hilton, began her career in South Australia and then headed for Europe, where she worked in a boutique hotel in Sussex, England. She returned to Adelaide ("the food and wine mecca of Australia"), where she heads a team of 36 chefs. Her style is influenced by the region's Mediterranean climate, Asian ingredients and the finest local produce.

Herbet Franceschini recently celebrated his 30th year with the Hilton International. German-born, he worked in the Americas before coming to Australia to open the Sydney Hilton as Executive Chef in 1974. As Executive Chef of the Brisbane Hilton since 1986, he launched an on-going Guest Chef program, bringing in top Australian and international chefs, and was host chef at Queensland's inaugural Masterclass Weekend in 1995.

Werner Kimmeringer first donned a cook's apron in his native Bavaria at the age of 14. Since then, he worked in restaurant kitchens around the world, returning to Europe in 1983 and joining the Hilton in Brussels. His innovative work in Sydney Hilton's San Francisco Grill won him awards, and since coming to the Melbourne Hilton in 1991, he has won further accolades as Chef of the Year in Victoria. He has traveled Australia extensively, collecting new ideas and ingredients.

Allan Koh, Executive Chef of Melbourne's trend-setting East-West restaurant, Chinois, began his training in a Japanese restaurant in Kuala Lumpur, Malaysia, at the age of 15, moving on to a Vietnamese restaurant before coming to Australia in 1987. He joined Chinois in 1989, where he creates a distinctive style of food blending Asian and Western ingredients and cooking techniques.

Kurt Looser, Executive Chef of Sydney Hilton, began his career in Switzerland, honing his skills in London, Bermuda and the Bahamas before joining the Sydney Hilton in 1973. He moved to Parmelia Perth Hilton in 1979, then returned to Switzerland for 12 months. He was invited back to the Sydney Hilton as Executive Chef in 1981. His style of cuisine is "Australian and international," using imagination and well practiced methods of preparation with the best of local produce.

Ashley Mackevicius is one of Australia's leading food photographers, whose images of food have graced numerous cookbooks and magazines both in Australia and overseas. He is also the food photographer for this book. His love of food and cooking brings with it a style that is distinctive, modern and very much in tune with contemporary Australian cuisine. He looks forward to showing the rest of the world that Australian food is distinctive and has a quality which ranks it among the world's best.

Tess Mallos, born in Australia of Greek parents, began her career as a consultant in the food industry. She has worked as a cookbook author and food writer for 35 years, as well as being involved in consumer education, advertising and TV cooking program. The best known of her many cookbooks are *The Greek Cookbook, The Complete Middle East Cookbook, The Filo Pastry Cookbook* and *Mediterranean Cooking*.

Christine Manfield, co-owner and

chef of the highly acclaimed Paramount Restaurant in Sydney, worked with Philip Searle at Oasis Seros in Sydney and at the Petaluma Restaurant in Adelaide before venturing into business with partner Margie Harris. Her food is intrinsically Australian in technique, style and presentation, with its original blend of assertive flavors and harmonious textures.

Bill Marchetti began training as a chef in his native Italy at the age of 13. He came to Australia in 1968 and in 1984 took over the Latin Restaurant in a famous Melbourne location which has housed an Italian restaurant for more than a century. He regards himself as "a northern Italian traditionalist" in style and calls Australia "Italy's 22nd region."

Paul Merrony, who was born in Tasmania, trained in the famous Berowra Waters Inn before working as a chef in London and Paris. Since returning to Australia in 1987, he has attracted an enthusiastic following and has won a number of awards. At his Sydney restaurant, Merrony's, he prepares what he terms "new French cooking in Australia."

Damien Pignolet, a second-generation Australian of French origin, trained in Melbourne, where he ran a cooking school and wrote articles for a culinary magazine. He moved to Sydney in 1978 as Executive Chef of Pavilion on the Park. After work-

ing in a number of other top restaurants, he and his partner established Bistro Moncur, where Pignolet produces "an Australian interpretation of French cuisine" and continues teaching through his appearances as a guest chef in other Australian cities.

Dietmar Sawyere comes from a family of Swiss restaurateurs, and began working for the Savoy in London at the age of 16. He has worked in some of the world's most exclusive hotels and restaurants since, and won a number of awards. Appointed Executive Chef of the Regent in Melbourne in 1988, he came to Sydney 4 years later and set up Forty One Restaurant, where he concentrates on "bringing back reality to food."

Charmaine Solomon is best known as the woman who brought Asian cooking into Western kitchens with her cookbooks, particularly *The Complete Asian Cookbook*. Born in Sri Lanka, her Dutch Burgher family was renowned for their cooking skills, as was her mother's family in Burma and India. She has lived in Australia for 35 years, sharing her knowledge through the printed medium and TV.

Michael Symons, author of *One Continuous Picnic: A History of Eating in Australia* and *The Shared Table: Ideas for Australian Cuisine*, is completing further titles on the subject of food. He instigated the Symposiums of Australian Gastronomy in Adelaide

in 1984 and, inquiring into the peculiar absence of gastronomy from the Academy, completed a Ph.D. in the sociology of cuisine at Flinders University of South Australia in 1991.

Alla Wolf-Tasker, born in Austria of Russian parents, arrived in Australia as a baby and determined at an early age to pursue a career as a chef. After working in restaurants in Australia and Europe, she established a successful cooking school in Melbourne and, in 1993, opened the Lake House in the scenic Victorian countryside. She sees her cuisine as being firmly regionally and seasonally based, with emphasis placed on small local rural suppliers, yet also having a certain city sophistication and drawing on traditions from many parts of the world.

Tetsuya Wakuda, who was born in Tokyo, worked in hotels and restaurants there before coming to Australia in 1982. He immediately obtained a position in one of Sydney's top restaurants. In 1986, he opened a restaurant known as Ultimo's and then began what is now regarded as one of Australia's top restaurants, Tetsuya's, in 1989. Tetsuya creates dishes that enhance rather than alter the flavor of the main ingredients, blending Western cooking methods and ingredients with Japanese sensibilities and flavorings.

Index